Sob Sister
Journalism

Recent Titles in
Contributions to the Study of Mass Media and Communications

Transnational Media and Third World Development: The Structure and
Impact of Imperialism
William H. Meyer

Predictions of Public Opinion from the Mass Media: Computer
Content Analysis and Mathematical Modeling
David P. Fan

Papers for the Millions: The New Journalism in Britain, 1850s to 1914
Joel H. Wiener, editor

EFE: Spain's World News Agency
Soon Jin Kim

Media Freedom and Accountability
Everette E. Dennis, Donald M. Gillmor, and Theodore L. Glasser, editors

Choosing the News: The Profit Factor in News Selection
Philip Gaunt

Muckraking and Objectivity: Journalism's Colliding Traditions
Robert Miraldi

The News as Myth: Fact and Context in Journalism
Tom Koch

Cold War Rhetoric: Strategy, Metaphor, and Ideology
Martin J. Medhurst, Robert L. Ivie, Philip Wander, and Robert L. Scott

Foreign Policy and the Press: An Analysis of *The New York Times'* Coverage
of U.S. Foreign Policy
Nicholas O. Berry

Sob Sister
Journalism

PHYLLIS LESLIE ABRAMSON

Contributions to the Study of Mass Media and Communications, Number 23

GREENWOOD PRESS
New York • Westport, Connecticut • London

Library of Congress Cataloging-in-Publication Data

Abramson, Phyllis Leslie.
    Sob sister journalism / by Phyllis Leslie Abramson.
       p. cm.—(Contributions to the study of mass media and
communications, ISSN 0732–4456 ; no. 23)
    Includes bibliographical references and index.
    ISBN 0–313–26513–5 (lib. bdg. : alk. paper)
    1. Women journalists—United States. 2. Nesbit, Evelyn,
1884–1967. 3. White, Stanford, 1853–1906. 4. Thaw, Harry Kendall,
1871–1947. I. Title. II. Series.
PN4888.W65A37   1990
070′.92′273—dc20   90–36637

British Library Cataloguing in Publication Data is available.

Library of Congress Catalog Card Number: 90–36637
ISBN: 0–313–26513–5
ISSN: 0732–4456

First published in 1990

Greenwood Press, 88 Post Road West, Westport, CT   06881
An imprint of Greenwood Publishing Group, Inc.

Printed in the United States of America

It is only the women whose eyes have been washed clear with tears who get the broad vision that makes them little sisters to all the world.

Dorothy Dix

Contents

Acknowledgments

This is, in many ways, a collaborative effort and would not have come to pass without the help, love, and encouragement of my wonderful family and friends. Especially, I would like to thank Dr. Robert Wheeler, Professor Emeritus, Emory University, for his many hours of guidance, June Mann for her sage advice, and the interlibrary loan staff at the Robert Woodruff Library, Emory University, who provided assistance and support in locating the obscure books, pamphlets, and newspapers needed for my research.

Finally, I want to thank my children, Peter and Julie, for their constant enthusiasm and my husband, Norman, for his love and support throughout the research and writing of this book. It is so great to be married to your best friend.

Sob Sister
Journalism

Chapter 1

Introduction

Every now and then an event occurs that in itself is of limited interest or importance but somehow captures the imagination and fascination of the public. Whether or not it attracts vast popular attention depends mainly on two factors: whether the public mood and climate are such that the event will be of great appeal and, more important, whether the press and other media feel that they can capitalize upon it. If the press decides that the incident is going to sell copy and especially if there is enormous initial public response, it will make sure that interest does not wane. For as long as curious readers buy the newspaper, the newspaper will continue to provide information, often irrelevant and unimportant, to satisfy this curiosity. Occasionally the press coverage and journalistic style become the focus of attention and the event merely a catalyst by which the journalistic style is propagated. Sometimes journalists rather than remaining impartial, colorless, factual transmitters of news, become celebrities themselves.

So it was that on the night of June 25, 1906, the public mood and climate were ripe and the press ready and eager for a "hot story." A steamy summer had descended upon New York City. Torpor and boredom lay heavily on people as it usually does before the "official" start of summer activities on July 4. Newspaper headlines would discuss nothing more interesting or entertaining than "John D. Rockefeller's new French wig was held up at the pier because the customs duties had not been paid."[1] Suddenly shots rang out in a restaurant in midtown Manhattan. A murder had been committed. On the surface the facts seemed prosaic and a bit timeworn. A somewhat deranged and insanely jealous man had murdered his wife's lover. But these were not just any three people involved in the eternal love triangle. The victim was Stanford White, a famous architect and womanizer; the murderer was Harry K. Thaw, the wealthy scion of a famous and influential family; and the woman was Evelyn Nesbit, the beautiful, somewhat innocent young woman who was victimized by both men. The public responded immediately and tenaciously. For the next several months, a conversation that did not include a discussion of this crime of the decade was unusual. The press, taking full advantage of the atmosphere that had been created, and the public's clamoring for every last detail no matter how trivial, gave this murder and the subsequent trial constant and unrelenting front-page exposure. Three famous newspapers assigned the story to four woman journalists who they felt could most adequately satisfy the readers' hunger for in-depth, emotional, heartrending, yes, even tear-producing reportage. Therefore, during the trial, seated prominently at a table in the front of the courtroom, these four women provided an avid readership with a daily dose of copy that was so mawkish and so soppy that only those who were unusually stalwart or unconscionably insensitive could keep from shedding a tear. Thus, the so-called sob sisters were born and sob sister journalism was created. This book deals with the origin of sob sister journalism. New York City, then as now, was a paradox. On the one hand it was a microcosm of human existence reflecting the life-style, problems, and thinking of the country as a whole. On the other, there was a uniqueness, a particular ambience that provided a suitable setting for this crime of the decade and the "trial of the century" that followed.

The fin de siècle witnessed a tremendous upsurge in the development of industrial centers. This trend toward industrialization was accompanied by a shift in demography to the cities. Simultaneously, a great flow of immigrants descended upon Ellis Island, seeking safety, happiness, and prosperity in America, the "land of opportunity." Many, if not most, of these people met oppression, disappointment, and frustration.

The American political scene was also in a state of flux. With the assassination of President William McKinley and the subsequent presidency of Theodore "Teddy" Roosevelt, the Progressive Era was introduced, and its effect was felt throughout the nation. Suffrage, prohibition, muckraking, and anti-trust legislation were all popular new ideas.

Women on all social levels were facing changes in life-styles, expectations, and responsibilities. This led to a great deal of confusion about women's role in the house and at the workplace. Factories were filled with lower-class women who were inexperienced and exploitable. Middle-class women were seeking a college education and posing a threat in established male areas of endeavor. Women of the upper classes were no longer satisfied to be "lady of the manor." The Victorian perception of womanhood was fading fast.

The press, too, was undergoing profound changes. There was a shift in emphasis from editorial comment and preoccupation with affairs of the government to wider fields of news and human interest. Like the Penny Papers of the early 1930s, yellow journalism gave readers a glittering show featuring articles on crime, sex, disasters, and wars. Everything seemed to be sensationalized in pictures, type, and innuendo. The newspaper became a medium of escape entertainment.

Yellow journalism was distinguished by its showmanship. Banner headlines stretched across the page. There was lavish use of pictures and a Sunday supplement included colored comics. On one occasion the supplement was printed in gold and scented throughout with rare perfume.

The yellow press made many positive contributions to the flow of American life and to the development of popular, democratic journalism. Though many outlandish tactics were employed to get attention and increase readership, they did readjust journalism from the Victorian era to the new industrial and urban age.

NOTE

1. Frederick Collins, *Glamorous Sinners* (New York: Macmillan, 1932), p. 2.

Chapter 2

An American Profile: 1900–1910

INDUSTRIALIZATION AND IMMIGRATION

The face of America changed with astonishing speed during the nineteenth century. Rural society gave way to urban, farms to industry.

By 1900 fewer than four workers in ten were in agriculture; American industry produced 31.9 percent of the world's coal, 34.1 percent of its iron, and 36.7 percent of its steel.[1] The businessman became the most important figure in society. The very rich wielded immense power. They included merchants like John Wanamaker of Philadelphia and Marshall Field of Chicago, railroaders like Edward H. Harriman, and the Armours and Swifts who bought most of the livestock of the Middle West. Tobacco production boomed, and four-fifths of all production was controlled by John Buchanan Duke of North Carolina.[2] Such magnates paid the wages of millions of workers and through purchases of raw products affected the livelihood of most families in the country.[3]

Those creating or enlarging industries or transportation had to go where the money was—to the great investment banks such as Kuhn, Loeb and Company and J. P. Morgan, who possessed billions for investment. These private bankers initially undertook corporate management to protest railroad loans and investments. Gradually, they began to believe firmly that monopolies represented the only source of order in mature capitalistic society.[4] Though they floated some of the largest bond issues, they would do so only when guaranteed the power to see that the funds were used prudently. J. P. Morgan's guiding principles were that "the interests of the nation and of the investing public were identical, that all businesses should be operated with primary regard for stockholders as a community, that control should be vested in men of character and that he, better than anyone else, could judge character."[5]

The financial boom that had started in 1897 suddenly came to a halt in 1907 when Frederick A. Heinze, with money from Montana copper operations, bought the Mercantile National Bank in New York City. Using its assets to back his stock speculation proved to be a poor gamble for the bank when one of Heinze's bigger investments failed. Questions about the soundness of his bank arose, and a run to withdraw funds began prompting concern about the soundness of other banks. This caused worried depositors to withdraw funds. The Knickerbocker Trust Company was forced to close its doors. The stock exchange faltered in March 1907.[6] There was no money available to buy offered stock.[7]

J. P. Morgan put "experts to work" assessing the strengths and weaknesses of the institutions in greatest danger. To some banks he lent great sums of money and, in addition, arranged for a $25 million fund to finance security purchases and bolster the stock exchange.[8] The Panic of 1907 was cushioned and in the end Morgan was to make large sums on the money he lent. Many of the smaller speculators and capitalists, unable to survive the financial crisis, saw their holdings taken over by larger interests. This resulted in a scramble for the nation's wealth, resulting in the formation of two financial giants—Standard Oil and the House of Morgan.[9] Though rivals, they managed to work together harmoniously.

The close intimate relationship between the employer and employee was quickly passing with the demise of small industry and corporation growth. The American work scene at the fin de siècle numbered a work force of 30 million men and women, poorly paid with work hard to come by. The average work week was fifty-nine hours, the average rate of pay less than ten dollars a week, though an eighty-four-hour week was not unheard of in the steel industry. John A. Ryan, an economist, concluded in 1906 that 60 percent of the adult male workers earned too little to maintain a family. Most of the more than 10 million immigrants in America by 1910 held the worst of the jobs, with the longest hours and the lowest rates of pay, largely because few had a trade and fewer a command of English.[10]

The immigrants arriving after 1890 were from Eastern and Southern Europe, especially Russia, Poland, and Italy. Most had agrarian backgrounds.[11] Those from Ireland were less likely to be peasants and more likely industrial workers. They, by and large, settled at a point of entry such as Boston or New York and worked in the industrial or mercantile sectors. This new wave of immigration reached a peak after the turn of the century. In the first six years of the twentieth century the number of immigrant admissions rose above the million mark. The total number of entrants between 1890 and 1914 was more than 16 million.[12] One-third of these newcomers were women.[13]

The American environment was different to the immigrants. As strangers, they had difficulty locating themselves. They had lost the polestar giving them their bearings. Only when they could feel themselves settled in their new context would they regain an awareness of direction.[14]

Peasants who had arrived earlier hoped to buy and live on small farms in America. They quickly found the Western frontier filled and the price of land very high. They had come too late and were too poor to buy farms. Their alternative was to spend the rest of their lives in the city, joining those already settled in the port and urban areas. From 1880 to 1890 the urban population of the United States grew from 14 million to 22 million.[15] New York, Chicago, and Boston became huge urban areas.

Factory owners enjoyed a steady supply of new workers. Immigrant women became part of the lowest class of industrial labor. They worked in mills and factories that produced textiles, clothing, and appliances.[16] Mothers of small children sought ways to work at home. Usually this was in the manufacturing trades, rolling cigars; sewing millinery, shirtwaists, or underwear; or making artificial flowers. "Homework was controlled by a contractor, or by a middle-man who picked up bundles of cut garments from outside manufacturing shops, and farmed them out to workers."[17] Contractors would often buy whole blocks of tenements and lease them to families who worked at finishing garments, morning, noon, and night. This was the birth of the sweatshop. Working steadily for twelve hours a day female workers would earn approximately three dollars per week.[18]

Providing rooms for boarders was another source of income for immigrant women. Since male immigrants most often sought room and board, the "boarder-wife-husband triangle" often became a discordant theme, sometimes causing disrupted marriages.[19] Marriages were also tested when alcoholism, prostitution, juvenile delinquency, and mental illness manifested themselves as signs of pressure.

To add to pressure on marriage and family was the inordinately high birth rate among the immigrant women. For every thousand married women of American birth in 1910 there were 3.396 births; for foreign-born the figure was 4.275 births per thousand.[20] In some urban areas three out of five babies died in their first year.[21] The tenements and slums were breeding places for disease. Tuberculosis, pneumonia, diphtheria, and other childhood diseases were common. Epidemics, blamed on close quarters, were common. Few immigrants had money for doctors, and women were often called to nurse the whole neighborhood.

Women provided support in many ways. When faced with new problems, the first-generation immigrant looked inward to his own kind for help. Self-help groups emerged in the neighborhood and in the factory.

Objecting to a lack of craftsmanship, continuous stress, and poor working conditions, women spoke out about how they were hired in "female only" positions in unskilled jobs where wages were sex segregated.[22] Most female factory workers were paid by the piece rather than being assured of a fixed salary.[23]

One woman interviewed by the magazine *The Independent* told what it was like to work in a garment factory in Brooklyn, New York.

I get up at half-past five o'clock every morning and make myself a cup of coffee on the oil stove. I eat a bit of bread and perhaps some fruit and then go to work.

At seven o'clock we all sit down to our machines, and the boss brings to each one the pile of work that he or she has to finish during the day, what they call in English their "stint." This pile is put down beside the machine and as soon as the shirt is done it is laid on the other side of the machine. . . . The machines go like mad all day, because the faster you work the more money you get. Sometimes in my haste I get my finger caught and the needle goes right through it. It goes so quick though that it does not hurt much. I bind the finger up with a piece of cotton and go on working. We all have accidents like that. . . . Sometimes a finger has to come off. . . . All the time we are working the boss walks about examining the finished garments and making us do them over again if they are not just right. So we have to be careful as well as swift.[24]

Unskilled work never afforded women a living wage. They were the cheapest pool of workers in the labor force, receiving one-half to one-third the wages of working men.[25]

During this same time the gross national product more than doubled and the product per capita went up by about 60 percent.[26] The nation's supplies of fuel and minerals were keeping pace with manufacturing demands. There was no danger that a lack of raw supplies would hamper industrial growth. Ownership in industry was becoming increasingly concentrated with the greatest power and wealth belonging to a few. The contrast between wealth and poverty, employer and employee was extreme.

It soon became apparent that economic improvement for the worker could be attained only through collective action. The workers' cause became the cause of Samuel Gompers, Elizabeth Gurley Flynn, and Rose Schneiderman among many others. They were in the forefront of labor organization.

Skilled workers, many native-born, feared losing their jobs through mechanization or replacement by cheaper unskilled immigrant labor. They organized exclusive craft or trade unions. These unions flourished, but skilled workers were reluctant to give up their individual power and join a national labor organization that would include unskilled labor. The skilled workers' resistance to the nationalizing of union activities coupled with the determination of employers to use every weapon at their disposal to halt national unionization resulted in organization of only a small percentage of the total labor force. The skilled laborers retained their craft unions and eventually did organize under the American Federation of Labor which was initially closed to unskilled laborers. At the end of the first decade of the twentieth century, out of a total labor force of about 25 million, only 2.4 million belonged to national unions, leaving the great majority of American workers without the means of self-protection.[27]

Employers continued to economize on payrolls. Believing that labor was the most manageable element in the cost of production, they strove to keep wages as low as possible. During the early 1900s many workers and intellectuals empathized with the plight of the unskilled laborer. Women were a significant proportion of this labor group. The empathizers encouraged a drastic change in the economic system. They rejected the American capitalist system and allied themselves with Eugene Debs, a leader of the American Socialist party.[28] They envisioned a cooperative society in which "workers would share in the profits of their labors and government would assume ownership of industry."[29] Many tried to convince Samuel Gompers and the American Federation of Labor (AFL) to abandon their craft-union policy and include unskilled laborers. Gompers vehemently fought socialism.

Believing that women could never receive equal opportunity and treatment in capitalistic America, radical feminists also "spoke for a socialist revolution, a radical redistribution of wealth, and an end to poverty."[30] Among them was Elizabeth Gurley Flynn, who fervently believed that capitalist society would deprive women of equal opportunities. By the time she was fifteen, Flynn was on the street corners orating about the plight of women and women's causes.[31]

In 1905 Flynn joined Debs and other radical leaders to form the International Workers of the World (IWW). The IWW was aimed at recruiting unskilled labor, the rank and file, and the unorganized. The "wobblies," as they came to be called, were openly revolutionary, rejected capitalism, and summoned the workers to a class war.[32] Debs, opposing the violent tactics of the IWW, disavowed any support of the group. Flynn continued to share the IWW helm and traveled the country organizing workers. She frequently participated in strikes and was often arrested. Her union activities continued throughout her life.[33]

Another significant contributor to the trade union movement was Rose Schneiderman, who was instrumental in founding the International Ladies Garment Workers Union (ILGWU). It started as a small walkout of workers from the Triangle Shirtwaist Company, one of the largest manufacturers of women's blouses in New York City.[34] Workers picketed daily, carrying banners proclaiming "We want bread and roses, too."[35] They wanted the right to organize and to bargain collectively with bosses for improved wages and working conditions. The Triangle Shirtwaist Company stationed prostitutes in front of its shop to fight off the pickets.[36] Though it began with one shop, by the time the strike was over, between 20,000 and 30,000 workers from other shirtwaist factories joined, changing the course of the labor movement and organizing more women than had ever been unionized before.[37] The strike was "characteristic of all strikes in which women play an active part. It was marked by complete self-surrender to a cause, emotional endurance, fearlessness and entire willingness to face danger and suffering. The strike at times seemed to be an expression of the woman's movement rather than labor movement."[38] The strike eventually led to the famous "Protocol in the Dress and Waist Industry" negotiated by Louis Brandeis.[39] This was the first, albeit biased, contract between labor and management. It formalized the trade's division of labor by gender. Men were assigned to more skilled jobs, with the lowest-paid working male earning more than the highest-paid female.[40]

Women's demands for health and safety regulations were ignored, resulting in the tragic loss of 146 lives in the Triangle Company fire of 1915.[41] The fire aroused the ire of other factory workers. Sympathetic workers in Lawrence, Massachusetts, mainly women and children, "poured into the streets to declare a strike."[42] The strike continued even though the strikers' funds were depleted. Food and fuel supplies diminished, and the strikers were facing starvation. Public reaction turned to the side of the workers. With the threat of a congressional investigation, mill owners decided to accept the strikers' demands, awarding a 5 to 20 percent wage increase, the largest amount to women and children.[43] Though this did represent some improvement in wages and working conditions, not until World War I did women in the labor force have an opportunity to perform in positions requiring skilled labor.

POLITICS

Progressivism was a reform movement that had its roots in the 1890s but came to a climax on the national level during the administrations of Theodore Roosevelt and Woodrow Wilson. It affected all areas of life including art, literature, religion, and education but was also "a political movement founded on the idea that the problems arising in an industrialized America could be solved only by expanding democracy and social justice."[44]

Historians who have studied progressivism disagree on the reason for its popularity. Some theorize that the progressive impulse came from those who found it difficult to adjust to the changes brought by the industrial age. Others see it as a moral crusade against sin and evil, while a third group feels that progressivism reflects belief that a strong government could correct evils.[45]

The movement included advocates of women's rights, businessmen angry over competition from the trusts, professional politicians who saw it as a means of gaining votes, and those empathetic with the sweatshop worker and child in the mill.[46] They sought to promote clean government and to end boss rule. They believed in progress and were certain that their efforts could improve the quality of life. Progressive literature abounded in exhortations to judge people by what they *did* and *were* rather than by what they *had* and *wore*.[47]

The moralistic attitude of the age made Americans receptive to verbal attacks on the professional politician and his life-style. In this mood of concern for more honest government and desire to restrict the size of the electorate to purify politics, Theodore Roosevelt found himself the dominant Republican figure, around whom factions formed and party fortunes revolved.[48]

Roosevelt was an ambitious, impatient, unpredictable Republican. A prominent politician for two decades, he had, on the surface, sound Republican credentials. His popularity and the absence of an alternative gave Roosevelt the vice presidential nomination on the McKinley ticket. The Republican hierarchy found that Roosevelt enjoyed a hold on the public mind and a capacity for winning votes.[49]

Though masterful on the campaign trail, Roosevelt was less successful with Congress and his party. His desire to strengthen executive power and reduce legislative responsibilities caused a steady deterioration of relations between Capitol Hill and the White House.

His first term was devoted to implementing and enacting the programs proposed by his predecessor, William McKinley, whose assassination catapulted Roosevelt into the presidency in September 1901. Though the tangible achievements during his first term were limited, he did emphasize the trust question, which gave public emotions a chance to vent themselves and provided a major element in building Roosevelt's popular standing.

"I am no longer a political accident," Roosevelt told his wife following his land-slide election in 1904.[50] The energies of his second administration were directed toward trust busting, including strong railroad legislation, child labor law reform, legislation preventing the "manufacture, sale or transportation [in foreign or interstate commerce] of adulterated or misbranded or poisonous or deleterious foods, drugs, medicines and liquors.[51] Powerful regulation in the area of conservation was also enacted, allowing an increase of the acreage of our national forests from 23 million acres to 194 million acres, creation of national parks, establishing sixteen national monuments, and setting aside fifty-one wildlife refuges.[52] Roosevelt's success in ceaselessly wooing reporters and subtly influencing the press also greatly contributed to a successful second term as president.

WOMEN

In order to understand women in the twentieth century it is necessary first to delineate the dominant ideology about women in the Victorian period and the basic notions about women's place and women's nature. The basic Victorian theme was the assumption that a woman's place was in the home as wife and mother, and the "lady" was the model for all women. Charlotte Perkins Gilman wrote of "woman as half the human race, mothers of all of it, cut off from their great work of world-raising by their position as private servants. Everyman requires one whole woman to minister to him."[53]

The home, considered the sphere in which a woman accomplished her most fitting work, was the place where she was expected to "minister to the personal and moral needs of her family, as well as seeing to their practical wellbeing; to nurse when they are sick; provide diversion when they are unhappy; remind them of religious truth when they are spiritually uncertain."[54] The home was also central to the maintenance of a women's sexual purity and

respectability. Only low and vulgar women had unnaturally vigorous or evident sexual desires. Respectable women felt little sexual
interest and submitted to marital duties "only in the hope of
motherhood."[55] Motherhood represented the height of a woman's
achievement, placing her higher on the "scale of being."[56] In
raising and training her family, it was felt, she would legitimately
hope to influence the moral development of society.

The attitudes and behavior of the lady became generalized and
established as the standards that a woman had to meet to demonstrate her womanliness and respectability. But working outside the
home meant that a woman was unprotected, subject to close
physical contact with strange men and to the orders of men who
were not her father or husband.[57] Among those elements of work
incongruous with being a lady were manual labor, publicity, inter-
action with people of lower standing, and personal service. The
most threatening aspect of the working world was the danger of
falling into impropriety and sexual irregularity.[58]

Major changes in thought and behavior toward women came in
the latter part of the nineteenth century. Urbanization and industrialization were proceeding at an increasing pace. Women were
following the migration pattern from country to city, from farm to
factory. At all economic levels women were breaking out of the
confines of the home and entering the public arena. For the
immigrant and lower-class women this process brought them into
jobs outside the home in domestic service, sweatshops, and factories.[59] The rate of female employment outside the home began to
rise from its Victorian nadir in the 1870s. Between 1880 and 1910
the proportion of adult females enrolled in the labor force rose from
14.7 to 24.8 percent.[60] For the wealthier women, increased leisure
time and education created opportunity to enter the professions and
invest energies in the cause of social justice, and women became
a major element in the Progressive reform movement. They were
instrumental in the formation of organizations that confronted
social issues from pornography to world peace.

Radical critics, such as the reform Darwinists, "challenged the
sanctity of social and economic institutions that confined women

to a limited sphere of influence."[61] One of the leading Darwinists was Charlotte Perkins Gilman, who wrote *Woman and Economics*, a critical assault on the economic basis of women's subordination to men. Launching into a radical assault on the "inequalities and inefficiencies" of contemporary marriage, she proclaimed that only a fundamental change in the economic specialization of the sexes could reorient the relationship between husband and wife to make true social progress possible.[62]

Major shifts were occurring in sexual and marital practices. A startling rise in the rate of illegitimacy and premarital intercourse, which had been falling throughout the nineteenth century, indicated increased sexual activity. More women than ever before in history were choosing not to marry.[63]

Opportunities for education expanded and drew middle-class women out of the home and into some professions.[64] By the end of the century females accounted for 40 percent of the graduates of American institutions with most moving into the job market.[65] Aside from factory workers, most employed women at the time were teachers, nurses, or librarians.[66]

Some of these educated middle-class women were horrified by multiplying slums, contaminated food and water, and unhealthy conditions in which the poor labored. They formed women's clubs and played an important role in securing protective legislation for child labor, pure food and drugs, and conservation.[67] They devoted themselves to serving others in missions overseas and in settlement houses in the ghettos. The most famous settlement house was Hull House, founded in Chicago by Jane Addams, a wealthy, well-educated socialite, who strongly felt that the dependence of classes on each other was reciprocal.[68] Another was the Henry Street settlement established on the Lower East Side of New York City by Lillian Wald, a nurse, who also started the public school nursing program.[69] Lillian Wald felt that the neighborhood households (settlement houses) were so successful because of the "natural simplicity of the household and the happy relations that grew out of this kind of living together."[70]

Women's suffrage was also becoming the focus of the women's movement. In 1890 various factions of the suffrage movement banded together in the National American Women Suffrage Movement under the presidency of Elizabeth Cady Stanton.[71] From 1890 to 1910 the organization continued to secure women's suffrage on a state-by-state basis.[72] Only a handful of states provided for equal suffrage. The Nineteenth Amendment was not recommended until the presidency of Woodrow Wilson when it was suggested as a wartime measure in response to women's total support of World War I.[73]

Middle-class women continued in their roles as social reformers well into the twentieth century. Upper-class women also found old roles disappearing. Industrial society had replaced their productive roles, increasing leisure time. Food stuffs, such as canned goods and bakery products, were now prepackaged and readily available; clothes could be purchased off the rack. Some, like their middle-class sisters, went to college and into reform movements to find more active roles for themselves. With greater leisure they thought more about sexuality and began to ask more from marriage than a Victorian sense of duty. Intimacy, passion, and spontaneity became part of the love-making scenario.

Unlike their Victorian counterparts, twentieth-century women were included when their husbands sought evening entertainment. This often included a visit to the roof garden theater, a new phenomenon, where the highest-salaried vaudeville performers appeared in a private, intimate atmosphere, thus giving the evening a touch of naughtiness. For the most part the general public was not permitted at the establishment, and the look of the cabaret changed from "joint" to "lobster palace." The change in decor allowed rich urbanites a place to enjoy more "risque entertainment and dancing in public."[74]

American women of the respectable class were beginning to enjoy an informal social life. They ventured into areas "where neither the activities of the entertainers or the behavior of the customers could be considered entirely respectable or predictable by nineteenth-century standards."[75] Many saw this as a threat to proper urban life and Victorian values. For the first time respectable women were mixing with people of "unspecified moral character," and for the first time men and women enjoyed a "public, informal atmosphere together."[76]

Reformers saw a decline in true womanhood with the advent of cabarets and cafes. Here they saw respectable women seeking passion through dance where "close physical contact and body expressions connoted loss of self-control."[77] The cabaret posed a threat to the role of domesticity. Women had been considered pure, religious, and moral, and their participation in the cabaret was viewed as the abandonment of civilized restraint. The new amusements "broke with nineteenth-century traditions by bringing men and women together in pleasurable, fast environments leaving behind class- and sex-segregated entertainments of earlier periods."[78] Women were seeking a new identity. They were no longer restrained by the traditional roles experienced by earlier generations. The home was no longer their only domain. Upper-class men changed their roles and concurrently their attitudes to accommodate the new woman and wife.

This change in traditional roles was also occurring at the lower-class level. One third of the 35 million Europeans who left their homelands between 1820 and 1920 to settle in America were women. Most of the new arrivals were peasants. Everything in a peasant woman's life including "work, marriage, child rearing and ways of thinking and behaving followed a prescribed pattern handed down from generation to generation."[79]

Peasant society followed strict patriarchal lines. Though woman exerted significant power within the family, they had no separate legal existence from husbands or fathers. Property was passed from father to son.[80] Women's power existed in the emotional, spiritual, and moral influence they had on the family. Upon their arrival in the New World, immigrant women did not work in heavy industry but instead became part of the lower class of industrial labor. They worked in mills and factories producing textiles, clothing, and appliances.

First-generation immigrants clung to values and customs prac-
ticed in the old country. This helped to provide a sense of continuity
and meaning when faced with new experiences in America. The
children of immigrants did not tenaciously resist change as did
their parents. This process often led to painful conflicts between
parent and child. A gap often developed particularly between
mother and child.

In the old country the concept of individuality and "personal
happiness" was meaningless. Women and men were defined by
their place in the family and a view of the self was nonexistent.[81]
Young women who had arrived in America as children or were
born in the United States saw themselves as individuals, separate
from their families. It was more difficult for immigrant women to
maintain traditional relationships with their children than with
their husbands. When the children were young and completely in
their mothers' care, they could be raised in the old ways. When the
children went off to school, this was no longer possible. The
children were more apt to listen to their American teachers than to
their mothers, who spoke with a foreign accent. The children
would usually choose to answer in English their parents' Italian or
Polish questions.[82] Children would point out the wrongs of their
parents.

When daughters reached adolescence, mothers could no longer
raise them in the old way. In leaving behind the European past,
mothers realized that their daughters were also leaving them.
Mothers forbade their daughters from going to dance halls, but the
daughters went anyway. Some exerted their own will when it came
time to choose a marital partner. Parents from the old country
whose own marriages had been arranged thought it "madness to
allow daughters to choose for themselves."[83] In the old country
marriage was an economic and social institution, not a romantic
one. Their American daughters could not understand marrying
someone they did not love.

Breaking their ties with the past was a very painful experience
for most daughters. They spent most of their time fighting family
restrictions for female independence. This rebellion led to a feeling

of rootlessness in the new world—a sense of loss of family and community.

Anzia Yezierska in the book *Children of Loneliness* describes this feeling:

> I'm one of the millions of immigrant children, children of loneliness, wandering between worlds that are at once too old and too new to live in. . . . I can't live with the old world and I'm yet too green for the new. I don't belong to those who gave me birth or to those with whom I am educated.[84]

Becoming Americanized caused great self-doubt and self-criticism, but the same process made these young women feel proud and self-assured.

PRESS

Gilded Age journalism, as this period is called, was fascinating and important. It may be called the second revolution in American newspapers.

The first revolution in American journalism occurred when the penny press was established in the 1830s and extended its influence throughout the country.[85] These newspapers were popular and cheap. With new distribution methods, (selling individual copies on the street) publishers of the penny press reached thousands of new readers.[86]

The second revolution in the United States press pattern was begun by Charles A. Dana of the *New York Sun*, extended by Joseph Pulitzer of the *New York World*, and brought to a climax by William Randolph Hearst of the *San Francisco Examiner* and the *New York Journal*. Two phenomena are outstanding in the period between the years 1892 and 1914: the "pyrotechnical outburst of yellow journalism"[87] and the large circulation and profits of leading papers.

While the name "yellow journalism" or "yellow press" for the new kind of journalism became a term of contempt, these papers made a great contribution to American life and the development of popular democratic journalism.[88] Gilded Age journalism was first called "Yellow Journalism" in 1893, when, for the first time, newspapers used colored comics or colored features. Richard F. Outcault, cartoonist employed by the *New York Sunday World*, "painted a bright yellow dress on the leader of the Hogan Alley Gang."[89] This "one-tooth ragamuffin," the "yellow kid," was pictured in situations connected with the events of the day in New York.[90] When Outcault, creator of the "Yellow Kid," left the *New York World* for the Hearst Papers, the "Yellow Kid" became twins because Pulitzer hired George B. Luks, later a painter of great merit, to continue the "Yellow Kid" in the Sunday edition of the *New York Journal*.[91] The cartoon was such a success that it became the symbol of the Pulitzer-Hearst brand of sensational journalism.

The format for the papers of the day was developed by Morrill Goddard, who, at different points in his career, worked for both Pulitzer and Hearst.[92] The formula included "a few pages of news and editorial in the usual style, plus page spreads or double-pages devoted to exaggerated and sensationalized versions of chosen phases of science or pseudo-science, plus a similar play of some crime material, plus some pages of stage comments with emphasis on legs, plus advice to girls and lovers, the exploitation of some prominent literary or social figure, sports and society and comics."[93] The aggressive publisher, in order to improve distribution methods and increase circulation, built more automatic printing presses, used stereotyping to produce duplicate plates for printing newspapers more quickly and in greater quantities, and placed advertisements on large billboards and in other trade organs.[94]

Many of the newspaper techniques used today were established during this period. Two-column, three-column, and banner headlines stretching across front pages and inside pages were first introduced in the 1890s.[95] The use of pictures and Sunday supplements was introduced to modern journalism at this time.[96] Mott enumerates the most distinguishing techniques of yellow journalism: (1) scare-heads, in which excessively large type, printed in either black or red, screamed excitement, often about comparatively unimportant news, thus giving a shrill falsity to the entire makeup; (2) the lavish use of pictures, many of them without significance, inviting the abuses of picture-stealing and "faked" pictures; (3) impostures and frauds of various kinds, such as "faked" interviews and stories, misleading heads, pseudo-science, and a parade of false learning; (4) the Sunday supplement, with colored comics and superficial articles; and (5) more or less ostentatious sympathy with the "underdog," with campaigns against abuses suffered by the common people.[97]

The general effect was grotesque and vicious, and the more blatant and dishonest phases of yellow journalism flourished for little more than the first decade of the twentieth century. A study of the papers in the twenty-one large metropolitan centers in 1900 showed a third of them were considered distinctly "yellow."[98]

During the same period the press also changed as a social institution. Many of the newspapers caught the "social drift." They reflected the urban trends of American life and recognized the various classes in the city. The press became less rural and more a product of the urban areas. A great deal of the news reflected the cosmopolitan interest of leaders.[99]

The upper-income group, living in mansions and country show places, were the best educated. They chose newspapers that reflected cultural interests. The newspapers also catered to this group with political and economic news, serious editorial pages, book reviews, and a financial section. The middle-income group living in less expensive brownstones and apartments bought newspapers catering to their economic and psychological interests.

Many publishers recognizing the needs of the low-paid workers and families on relief, who occupied "cheerless tenements, with little air and poor facilities . . . began campaigns to establish funds for the poor, free medical service for the sick, free milk for the children and other human helps."[100]

To balance the campaigns and crusades on behalf of the poor there was a tendency to print more "fun."[101] Commercial entertainment and recreation were developing in the urban areas. Newspapers reported activities in the sports world. It came to be segregated on special pages, with special make-up pictures and new writing style.[102] "Throughout the bicycle craze of the 1890s many of the leading newspapers maintained special departments for wheelmen, giving news of cycle races, of the activities of wheelmen's clubs, and of manufacturers' new models."[103]

This period marked the rise of organized spectator sports. Baseball was the most popular and had become big business. Rivaling baseball was prize-fighting. The great event of the day was the emergence of John L. Sullivan, who was called champion of champions and dominated the ring at the turn of the century.[104]

The theater, also a form of recreation at the turn of the century, reflected a cross section of classes in American society and mirrored the problems of urban life. Vaudeville reflected the restlessness and rapid tempo of the day, with each act lasting five or ten minutes. Departments devoted to amusements grew with actresses and actors making good copy. Advertising from play producers and vaudeville entrepreneurs contributed to the newspapers' revenue.[105]

Advertisements also glowingly described products and services that women readers would purchase. With the development of urban living and the industrialization of America, women increasingly bought factory-made, store-bought merchandise. The family's ready-made clothes, formerly sewn in the home, were now being bought in stores. Canned goods and prepared cereal were obtained at the grocery. Bakeries became common, and fewer baked goods were made at home.[106]

Women achieved new legal and economic status during this period. They had more legal rights and control over their property, and thousands became rich through inheritance of fortunes. Other women were going to work, with an increase from 2.5 million working women in 1880 to 5 million at the turn of the century. As wage earners, their purchasing power quickly increased.

Growing leisure and advanced education levels made many women newspaper readers for the first time.[107] Publishers and editors, recognizing this trend, began to cater specifically to them with news, features, and pictures. The appeal was not limited to the women's pages; women were sent to cover the war in Cuba and in the Philippines, the prize fights, and the murder trials, so that they could bring the feminine point of view to their female readers.[108]

Women in all classes became more style-conscious and more aware of the world of fashion than ever before.[109] Women in the upper economic class, belonging to the growing high society, enjoyed formal affairs where they could display their beautiful, fashionable dresses. They were strongly influenced by news about clothes as well as advertisements in the daily press.[110] Retailers aimed their advertising at this group.[111]

The yellow journal, with its pictures, sensation, and easy editorials, brought the immigrant more and more into the newspaper audience. An observer in 1907 wrote:

> In the huge, intricate, swiftly growing structure of American society a complete new human foundation has wedged in beneath. A foundation of peasants suddenly brought from the home where papers were myths to the glaring cities of "extras". . . . A foundation that now slowly, word by word and line by line, is learning to read the news.[112]

Though the newspaper was not an automatic reflection of the Gilded Age, it was a social institution that responded positively and negatively to the period and influenced the attitudes and lives of the people.

NEW YORK CITY

Between 1880 and 1910 New York became the first American city to assume a modern character.[113] In 1897 New York City was the most populous city in the nation, surpassing Chicago by 400,000 people.[114] The Consolidation of 1898 converted the counties of Manhattan, Queens, Brooklyn, Bronx, and Richmond into boroughs that together boasted a population of 3,437,202 in 1900.[115]

Robert Van Wyck, a Tammany Hall candidate, was elected mayor of the consolidated boroughs. The metropolis needed political leadership to match its economic strength, but Van Wyck proved to be a poor choice. For the most part he used his power to "reward clubhouse hacks and nurture the organization."[116] No area of government suffered more under Van Wyck's rule than did the police department. There was an "understanding between business, politics and vice," each appreciating the greed and necessity of the other. Vice bosses replaced honest police officials, and when the Lexow Commission investigated the Police Department, it found an "established 'caste system' dedicated to the cohesion of public plunder."[117]

Special Session Court Judge William Travers Jerome systematically questioned police captains about protection of vice. Launching a series of "John Doe" raids, he won popular acclaim and was elevated to the position of Manhattan district attorney.[118]

New York City was to enjoy clean government for only six years under a Republican reformer candidate before Tammany Hall ruled once again. The election of George B. McClellan, Jr., the son of a Civil War general and a veteran of Tammany Hall politics, signaled the start of effective city administration.[119] His loyalty to Tammany politics lasted through his first mayoral candidacy, but lost its lustre when the Tammany Hall politicians launched a campaign of "foul words and bitter deeds" during the campaign of 1905 when McClellan faced William Randolph Hearst for mayor. McClellan won but was appalled by the campaign activities, and he dropped his Tammany supporters. From 1903 to 1909 he pursued an independent political course.[120] His administration was known for completing harbor improvements, beginning the municipal ferry service, expanding park and playground facilities, and, most of all, opening the subway system on October 27, 1904.[121] These new improvements were available for the 1,300,000 immigrants arriving at Ellis Island in 1907.[122] They became part of the teeming chaos of the tenement district where people were "packed together like herring in a barrel."[123]

Manhattan slums were slums at their most intense, contrasting sharply with other parts of the city. The Village as, Greenwich Village is affectionately called, by contrast was until the 1850s largely comprised of homes of wealthy families. It was not long before the area was infiltrated by "cosmopolites," wordly-wise people who loved to call themselves Bohemians.[124] This hub of creativity included among its residents Sidney Porter, popularly known as O. Henry, who lived on East 9th Street in the "House of Genius" and described the village setting in many of his stories.[125] Other tenants in this famous boarding house included Willa Cather, managing editor of *McClure's*,[126] two westerners, Theodore Dreiser and Sherwood Anderson, and Edna St. Vincent Millay, who had come to the Village to write poetry for which she later became famous, but who in the meantime was eking out a living as an actress.[127]

The middle classes were moving from Manhattan into the other boroughs. The Bronx, which Arnold Bennett described as "a place with a name so remarkable, it must itself be remarkable," afforded its inhabitants "four-room flats renting from $26, equipped with central heating and gas and electricity and supplied with a refrigerator, a kitchen range, a bookcase and a sideboard."[128]

Well-to-do people lived uptown in the Murray Hill section or on lower Fifth Avenue. In these districts one found "attached brownstones fronted by flights of steep stairs."[129] Farther up Fifth Avenue, between 50th and 80th streets, was "block after block of enormous, expensive and lavishly adorned private mansions" known as "millionaires' row."[130]

In 1898 New Yorkers were talking about a new free public library. Theaters were doing a flourishing business. The Shubert brothers had opened outlets for the stage. John Barrymore was the greatest actor, and George M. Cohan the brightest Broadway star.[131]

Popular culture reached out to all through the "cinema palace and neighborhood movie theatre."[132] The Fox and Loew chains reached the masses catering to the demand for dramatic fare. Mayor McClellan's city was an exciting and vital place to live when he retired in 1907 to a "life of scholarship at Princeton University."[133]

His successor was Supreme Court Judge William Gaynor, another Tammany Hall choice, an opinionated, irascible, and generally unstable individual—hardly conducive to easing the heated labor atmosphere of the period.[134] Workers were continuously using the strike as a weapon to obtain greater economic benefits, and unionization activities were intensifying across New York. The largest proportion of the working population was engaged in manufacturing and mechanical pursuits. Production within the city limits was valued at more than $1 billion dollars at the turn of the century, contrary to the popular belief that trade and finance set the tone of the city's economy, a belief fueled by the dominant portion of New York City financiers.[135] Among these financial giants was the triumvirate of J. P. Morgan, Sr.; James Stillman, head of the National City Bank of New York; and George F. Baker, president of the First National Bank of New York.[136] At the turn of the century New York City boasted the chief officers of more than a third of the largest industrial companies in the nation and of the country's four largest life insurance companies, with $7.5 billion of insurance in force, and assets of $2 billion.[137]

New Yorkers could observe tremendous physical changes in their city. The new "steel-cage structures stood out above the generally horizontal mass of the metropolis."[138] Buildings of enormous elevation seemed to spring up yearly. Macy's thirteen-story building opened on Thirty-Fourth Street in 1901.[139] The Flatiron building with its twenty-one stories was erected the following year.[140] The sixty-story Woolworth Building outclassed their predecessors, only to be eclipsed by the Pennsylvania Railroad Station, designed by Stanford White and completed in 1910.[141]

Manhattan had reached its greatest population figures in 1910, and then began a slow decline.

NOTES

1. Ernest May, *The Progressive Era*, vol. 9 (New York: Time-Life Books, 1964), p. 7.

2. Ibid.

3. Eli N. Evans, *The Provincials* (New York: Atheneum, 1973), p. 18.

4. Thomas Cochran and William Milke, *The Age of Enterprise: A Social History of Industrial America* (New York: Macmillan, 1942), p. 193.

5. May, *The Progressive Era*, vol. 9, p. 15.

6. Elizabeth Gurley Flynn, *I Speak My Own Piece: Autobiography of a Rebel Girl* (New York: Masses and Mainstream, 1955), p. 30.

7. May, *The Progressive Era*, vol. 9, p. 15.

8. Ibid., p. 16.

9. Ibid., p. 17.

10. May, *The Progressive Era*, vol. 9, p. 31–34.

11. June Sochen, *Herstory: A Woman's View of American History* (New York: Alfred, 1974), p. 213.

12. Handlin, *The Uprooted*, p. 68.

13. Carol Hymowitz and Michaele Weissman, *A History of Women in America* (New York: Bantam, 1978), p. 192.

14. Handlin, *The Uprooted*, pp. 85–86.

15. Hymowitz, *A History of Women in America*, p. 382.

16. Ibid., p. 193.

17. Ibid., p. 200.

18. Ibid., pp. 200–201.

19. Ibid., p. 202.

20. Ibid., p. 198.

21. Hymowitz, *A History of Women in America*, p. 198.

22. Ibid., p. 236.

23. Ibid., p. 236.

24. Ibid., p. 384.

25. Ibid., p. 239.

26. Handlin, *The Uprooted*, p. 74.

27. Ibid., p. 99.

28. Flynn, *I Speak My Own Piece*, p. 122.

29. Hymowitz, *A History of Women in America*, p. 245.

30. Ibid., p. 246.

31. June Sochen, *Movers and Shakers: American Women Thinkers and Activists 1900-1970* (New York: Quadrangle/The New York Times Book Co., 1973), p. 55.

32. Handlin, *The Uprooted*, p. 703.

33. Flynn, *I Speak My Own Piece*, p. 124.

34. Hymowitz, *A History of Women in America*, p. 249.

35. Sarah Eisenstein, *Give Us Bread But Give Us Roses* (London: Routledge and Kegan Paul, 1983), p. 32.

36. Hymowitz, *A History of Women in America*, p. 249.

37. Hymowitz, *A History of Women in America*, pp. 249–250.

38. Rosalyn Boxandall, Linda Gordon and Susan Reverby, *America's Working Women* (New York: Random House, 1976), pp. 192–193.

39. Handlin, *The Uprooted*, p. 205.

40. Hymowitz, *A History of Women in America*, p. 238.

41. Handlin, *The Uprooted*, p. 252.

42. Hymowitz, *A History of Women in America*, p. 255.

43. Ibid.

44. Allen F. Davis and Harold D. Woodman, *Conflict and Consensus in Modern American History*, 6th ed. (Lexington, Mass.: D. C. Heath, 1984), p. 251.

45. Ibid., p. 252.

46. May, *The Progressive Era*, p. 52.

47. Bailey Millard, "What Life Means to Me," *Cosmopolitan Magazine* 16 (1906): 516.

48. Lewis Gould, *The Progressive Era* (Syracuse, N.Y.: Syracuse University Press, 1982), p. 60.

49. Ibid., p. 61.

50. Edward Wagneknecht, *American Profile: 1900-1910* (Amherst, Mass.: University of Massachusetts Press, 1984), p. 15.

51. Ibid., p. 323.

52. Ibid., p. 324.

53. Gould, *The Progressive Era*, p. XV.

54. Eisenstein, *Give Us Bread But Give Us Roses*, p. 56.

55. Ibid., p. 57.

56. Ibid., p. 56.

57. Ibid., p. 68.

58. Ibid., p. 86.

59. Jean E. Friedman and William G. Shade, *Our American Sisters* (Lexington, Mass.: D. C. Heath, 1982), p. 322.

60. W. Elliot and Mary Brownlee, *Women and the American Economy: A Documentary History: 1675-1929* (New Haven, Conn.: Yale University Press, 1976), p. 3.

61. Friedman and Shade, *Our American Sisters*, p. 322.

62. Charlotte Perkins Gilman, *Women and Economics* (New York: Source Book Press, 1970), p. 58.

63. Friedman and Shade, *Our American Sisters*, p. 322.

64. Ibid.

65. Mary P. Ryan, *Womanhood in America: From Colonial Times to the Present* (New York: F. Watts, 1983), p. 201; Friedman and Shade, *Our American Sisters*, p. 323.

66. Friedman and Shade, *Our American Sisters*, p. 322.

67. Ibid.

68. Sochen, *Herstory*, p. 215; Jane Addams, *Twenty Years at Hull House* (New York: Macmillan, 1932), p. 91.

69. Inez Haynes Irwin, *Angels and Amazons, A Hundred Years of American Women* (Garden City, N.Y.: Doubleday, 1933), p. 160.

70. Wagneknecht, *American Profile: 1900-1910*, p. 8.

71. Aileen S. Kraditor, *The Ideas of the Woman Suffrage Movement* (New York: Columbia University Press, 1965), p. 4.

72. Andrew Sinclair, *The Better Half: The Emancipation of the American Woman* (New York: Harper and Row, 1965), p. 324.

73. Friedman and Shade, *Our American Sisters*, p. 325.

74. Eisenstein, *Give Us Bread But Give Us Roses*, pp. 75–76.

75. Ibid., p. 76.

76. Ibid., p. 77.

77. Ibid., p. 81.

78. Ibid., p. 85.

79. Hymowitz and Weissman, *A History of Women in America*, p. 192.

80. Ibid.

81. Ibid., p. 194.

82. Ibid., p. 209.

83. Ibid., p. 213.

84. Ibid., p. 215.

85. Sidney Kobre, *The Yellow Press and Gilded Age Journalism* (Talahassee, Fl.: Florida State University, 1964), p. iii.

86. Ibid.

87. Frank Luther Mott, *American Journalism: A History of Newspapers in the United States Through 250 Years, 1690-1940* (New York: Macmillan, 1947), p. 519.

88. Kobre, *The Yellow Press and Gilded Age Journalism*, p. iii.

89. Ibid., p. 52.

90. Ibid.; Wagenknecht, *American Profile: 1900-1910*, p. 199.

91. William Grosvenor Bleyer, *Main Currents in the History of American Journalism* (Boston: Little, Brown, 1927), p. 337.

92. Mott, *American Journalism*, p. 524.

93. Ibid.

94. Kobre, *The Yellow Press and Gilded Age Journalism*, p. v.

95. Ibid., p. iv.

96. Mott, *American Journalism*, p. 539.

97. Ibid.

98. Delos F. Wilcox, "The American Newspaper: A Study in Social Psychology," *Annals of the American Academy of Political and Social Science* 16 (July 1900): 56.

99. Kobre, *The Yellow Press and Gilded Age Journalism*, p. 13.

100. Ibid.

101. *New York Tribune*, 2 November 1902.

102. Mott, *American Journalism*, p. 579.

103. Ibid.

104. Kobre, *The Yellow Press and Gilded Age Journalism*, p. 15.

105. Ibid., p. 17.

106. Ibid., p. 18.

107. Ibid.

108. Mott, *American Journalism*, p. 599.

109. Sidney Kobre, *Development of American Journalism* (Dubuque, Iowa: W. C. Brown, 1969), p. 359.

110. Kobre, *The Yellow Press and Gilded Age Journalism*, p. 359.

111. Ibid., p. 20.

112. Mott, *American Journalism*, p. 599.

113. David Hammock, *Power and Society: Greater New York at the Turn of the Century* (New York: Russell Sage, 1982), preface.

114. George J. Lankevich and Howard B. Fures, *A Brief History of New York (New York: Associated Faculty Press, 1984), p. 197.*

115. Ibid., p. 132.

116. Ibid.

117. Ibid., p. 195.

118. Ibid., p. 196.

119. Ibid., p. 199

120. Ibid., p. 201.

121. Ibid., p. 200.

122. Ibid., p. 202.

123. Bayrd Still, *Mirror for Gotham* (Westport, Conn.: Greenwood Press, 1980), p. 267.

124. Maxwell F. Marcuse, *This Was New York: A Nostalgic Picture of Gotham in the Gaslight Era* (New York: Columbia University Press, 1948), p. 196.

125. Ibid., p. 117.

126. Allan Nevins and John A. Krout, *The Greater City: New York 1898-1948* (New York: Columbia University Press, 1948), p. 196.

127. Marcuse, *This Was New York*, p. 98.

128. Still, *Mirror for Gotham*, p. 268.

129. Nevins and Krout, *The Greater City*, p. 192.

130. Ibid.

131. Lankevich, *A Brief History of New York*, p. 203.

132. Still, *Mirror for Gotham*, p. 274.

133. Ibid., p. 734.

134. Lankevich, *A Brief History of New York*, p. 205.

135. Ibid.

136. Still, *Mirror for Gotham*, p. 265.

137. Nevins and Krout, *The Greater City: New York 1898-1948*, p. 180.

138. Still, *Mirror for Gotham*, p. 257.

139. Marcuse, *This Was New York*, p. 286.

140. G. E. Kidder Smith, *The Architecture of the United States* (New York: Anchor Books, 1981), p. 511.

141. Ibid., p. 523.

Chapter 3

Sob Sisters

WINIFRED BLACK

Birth to June 25, 1906

Winifred Black spent her last days "high up on Russian Hill in San Francisco, in a Spanish house that faced the Palace of Fine Arts."[1] She died on May 25, 1936, at the age of seventy-three.

One of the first of the Hearst stars, she initially met the publisher not in the city room but at a children's party when he came to her assistance in quieting a yelping dog. She was working at the *San Francisco Examiner* before Hearst left college and was identified with his beginnings in the newspaper business. Black was the one woman writer on his staff that he accepted into his inner circle.[2] She knew what it was like to have been "collected" by him. It filled her with profound gratitude but also with the knowledge that she had given her life and everything in it to his service.[3]

Born Martha Winifred Sweet on October 14, 1863, in Chilton, Wisconsin, the "statuesque, auburn-haired beauty" was raised in Chicago by a sister, Ada Celeste Sweet.[4] She was the fourth of the five children and youngest of three daughters of Benjamin Jeffrey Sweet and Lorin Loveland Sweet, both natives of upstate New York. Appointed United States pension agent for Chicago in 1869,

Sweet moved with his family to a farm west of the city. He died in January 1874, and his wife died four years later.[5] Black attended private schools in Lake Forest, Illinois, and in Northampton, Massachusetts, and after an unsuccessful attempt at a stage career in New York, she turned to journalism.

The move to journalism came almost by happenstance. "Her sister shared with the *Chicago Tribune* one of Winifred's letters in which an aspiring actress wrote of the trials and tribulation of stage life, describing her experience on tour with an amateur theatrical company."[6] The paper liked it and asked for more, but a family crisis intervened before she made the change to journalism as a lifelong career.

In 1889 Black traveled west in search of a runaway brother, whom she found safe on an Arizona ranch. A few days later she found herself in San Francisco in need of a job. Using skills she learned during her short theatrical career, Black acted like an experienced reporter when she applied for a job at the *San Francisco Examiner*. With some of the "invincibility" that followed her through life she managed to get on the staff.[7] She was hired by the conservative editor S. S. Chamberlain, an old-fashioned gentleman who wore grey pinstriped trousers, a cutaway coat, a wing collar, and spats to work.[8] Though she had no experience, perhaps Chamberlain on their first meeting recognized her potential and decided he could make a great newspaper woman out of her.

Her first assignment was to interview Elizabeth Bisland, who was sent around the world by *Cosmopolitan Magazine* in a sailing race against Nellie Bly.[9] Wanting her first article to be outstanding, she wrote it in beautiful, flowery prose, using a great many vivid adjectives. Chamberlain found it unacceptable and gave her a lesson in journalism that she was to "internalize and exemplify." "We don't want fine writing in a newspaper, Mrs. Black," he said. "There's a gripman on the Powell Street Line. He takes his car out at three in the morning, and while he's waiting for the signal he opens the morning paper. Think of him when you are writing a story. Don't write a single word he cannot understand and won't read." As he spoke, Chamberlain was ripping her story to bits and disposing of them in a wastebasket. "Now go rewrite your story," he said. "And this time give me newspaper style."[10] In a single lesson she had learned that in newspaper work, the style, not the story, is important.

In the 1890s it was still the custom for women reporters to write under pseudonyms. Winifred adopted the name Annie Laurie from the song her Scottish mother sang to her as a child.[11] Once started, her newspaper career was successful. She began during the era of street reporting, and Black was one of the best. She scored a number of exposés, scoops, and circulation-building publicity stunts.

Her next assignment was to investigate the city receiving hospital in San Francisco, with special attention to the treatment of women there. She dressed in old clothes and worn shoes, cut a "Plain Sewing Wanted" ad from a newspaper and tucked it into her shabby purse, and asked a doctor friend to drop belladonna into her eyes, so that the resulting glare would make her look of desperation all the more convincing. "Annie Laurie" described the following events:

> At 3 o'clock Friday afternoon a young woman, [as Annie Laurie described herself] alighted from a Market Street Car. . . . The street was crowded with vehicles and the clanging of the gripman's bells, the oath of the drivers and the swarm of pedestrians combined to make the scene one of confusion. . . . As the young woman walked up Kearny Street she put her hand to her head and almost closed her eyes as if from intense pain. Her struggle seemed to give up and she tottered up against a pile of bricks.
>
> A young man saw her pale face and closed eyes, and ran from a store nearby. Had it not been for the young man she would have fallen to the sidewalk. As it was she slumped into his arms. Another man ran to summon a policeman only to be told "I can't help. I can't leave my beat." He beckoned to another policeman who after a long delay had a covered wagon used to convey prisoners to the county jail. Two

policemen grabbed her arms and making no pretense of
carrying her, dragged her like a sack of grain too heavy to lift,
to where the wagon was waiting.

They swung her feet first into the wagon, jammed her into
a corner and . . . held her upright despite the fact that a
fainting woman may die if she is not laid down.

Her treatment at the San Francisco Receiving Hospital was no
better. "Annie Laurie" was greeted by a young doctor who, assum-
ing she was just another hysterical woman, grabbed her arm, had
another pull her head back, pried her mouth open and "forced some
nasty mixture of mustard water down my throat. Another doctor
noting her resistance suggested she be given a good thrashing."
Following her thrashing, she was left to fare for herself. The story
she wrote brought a governor's inspection, the firing of many on
the hospital staff, initiation of ambulance service to San Francisco,
and some improvement in the treatment of female patients.[12]

As one physician, Dr. McQuesten, stated, "For my part I am very
glad indeed this thing has happened and think that a debt of
gratitude is due to the *Examiner* and to the paper's plucky Annie
Laurie for making known what lies beneath the surface of this one
of our public institutions."[13]

This was the first in a long series of crusading stories. Other
exposés included "the undercover stunt in a Southern cotton mill;
a job at a local fruit cannery for twenty-six cents a day; interviews
with the proprietress of a brothel; and a role as a Salvation Army
angel at the Barbary Coast."[14]

In addition she wrote articles on "Little Jim," a crippled boy born
to a prostitute in the city prison hospital. These articles led to an
Examiner campaign to provide a ward for incurables at the San
Francisco Children's Hospital. For several years she directed this
and another of the newspaper's charitable projects. In another
crusade, she traveled to Molokai, the Hawaiian Island leper colony
with Sister Rose Gertrude, who "Annie Laurie" described as "a
bright eyed modest little woman who has achieved world wide
fame within the past few weeks by an extraordinary act of self

sacrifice in one of the most repulsive causes known to all human experience. Sister Rose Gertrude has left a charming home in England to bury herself forever among the wretched people of that dreadful colony, loathed of all mankind known as the leper settlement of Molokai."[15] Her articles brought an outpouring of financial support for the colony. The *New York Times* on May 26, 1936, reflected: "The poor, the oppressed and the helpless found in her a true friend and companion. The cause of the suffering and the helpless always elicited her sympathy and her aid."[16]

In 1895 when Hearst challenged Joseph Pulitzer on his own ground by purchasing the *New York Journal*, "Annie Laurie" moved east. The custom of *noms de plume* had begun to fade. In New York she wrote under the name of Winifred Black.[17] She briefly toured with William Jennings Bryan in 1896 and covered over 600 of his campaign speeches.[18]

She loved the West. Leaving New York in 1897 after a stay of only two years, she joined the *Denver Post*, rival of the *Journal* and the *World* in the field of yellow journalism. While maintaining an affiliation with the *Post*, she remained a Hearst feature writer. She got her greatest scoop on a special daring assignment for Hearst. A tidal wave crashed into Galveston, Texas, on September 8, 1900. Disguised as a boy to get through police lines, she became the first outside journalist, and the only woman reporter, to enter Galveston. A large part of the city had been washed away. The death toll was 7,000. It was a major disaster of American history. She got her story and managed to get through the line to file it. She urged her readers to send help quickly. Telegrams arrived announcing that four of the Hearst papers had relief trains on the way. She directed the relief works and distributed the $60,000 in cash that Hearst had sent. All told, she helped raise $350,000 for the survivors.[19]

Six years later the Thaw trial was to cover the front pages. Hearst again summoned Black to work as a feature writer for the Hearst International News Service.

DOROTHY DIX

Birth to June 25, 1906

Every day hundreds and sometimes thousands of troubled people laid their worries before Dorothy Dix. To all these troubled souls Dorothy Dix was just a name or a fuzzy picture in a daily newspaper. To her family and friends she was Elizabeth Meriwether, born on a 1,500-acre Tennessee plantation in Woodstock, Montgomery County, near the Kentucky border, on November 18, 1861.[20]

The Meriwethers were wealthy Southern gentry and kin to Meriwether Lewis, the explorer. "We were sent to school to Miss Alice's or Miss Jenny's, not because they were either trained or even qualified to teach, but because their fathers had been colonels under Beauregard, or had been killed at Shiloh, and somebody had to help the poor souls along."[21]

Elizabeth was taught the refinements of Southern ladyhood and encouraged to use the private family library. A confirmed bookworm by age twelve, Meriwether discovered the joys of writing. Her first major literary work "The Pleasures of Anticipation" created a sensation in her grammar school and remains a collector's item today.[22]

Following the death of his first wife, Maria Winston, William Douglas Meriwether married a strict stepmother, Martha Gilmer Chase.[23] Elizabeth's stepmother brought with her to the Meriwether home her brother, George O. Gilmer, "a man-about-Clarksville in his late twenties, a debonair gallant who dabbled a bit in business."[24] Elizabeth was flattered by the attention paid to her by this older man who was regarded as a man of the world.

At eighteen, as she wrote some time later, "I tucked up my hair and got married, as was the tribal custom among my people." Her marriage to Gilmer, ten years her senior, took place on November 12, 1888.[25] She expected to settle down to a conventional marital existence.

Almost from the start the marriage was a tragedy. George Gilmer showed signs of moodiness, difficulty getting along with others, and inability to keep a job. He was suffering from an incurable mental illness, the course of which was not to end until he died in a mental institution thirty-five years later.[26]

Elizabeth Gilmer was forced to go out and find some way to earn a living for herself and for him. She had never been taught any gainful occupation and was "reared in an atmosphere which stigmatized self-support in a woman as somehow shameful."[27] In the early years she managed to cope but eventually, due to stress, she had a nervous breakdown and in the early 1890s she went to the peaceful resort of Bay Saint Louis on the Mississippi Gulf Coast to recuperate.[28]

Fate intervened, and by chance she stayed next door to Mrs. E. J. Nicholson, the South's newly successful woman publisher and owner of the *New Orleans Picayune*. Gilmer showed Nicholson some newspaper features she had freelanced and sold her a story for three dollars. In 1894, at age thirty-three, Gilmer was hired as girl-friday for the *Picayune*'s editor, Major Nathaniel Burbank. Her salary was five dollars a week.[29]

She progressed from a cub reporter's gathering of vital statistics, to obituaries and birth notices and finally to her own column of advice to women. Originally entitled "Sunday Salad," the column was written realistically about the relationship of men and women. Her writing style was "crisp, breezy, even colloquial,"[30] avoiding the "romantic vaporing of the ear."[31]

The feature was an instant success. Alliterative pseudonyms, which were voguish in those days for gentlewomen, concealed their real names from the "stigma of the sordid newspaper world."[32] She chose Dorothy Dix and changed the name of her column to "Dorothy Dix Talks," the name it was to keep for fifty-five years.[33] From the start readers wrote laudatory letters about her column and gave invaluable suggestions for feature articles. She became a full-fledged reporter, and her salary increased from the original five dollars a week to fifteen dollars a week.[34]

Scouts of publisher William Randolph Hearst took notice of Dorothy Dix and offered her a position with the Hearst organization. Out of a sense of gratitude and loyalty to Major Burbank, Gilmer initially rejected the offer. Burbank died in 1901, and Gilmer felt free to leave the *Picayune*.

Her first assignment for the *New York Journal* was covering the front-page story of Carry Nation, the temperance leader, on her saloon-smashing tour of Kansas. She found Carry a "queer, frowzy, fat unromantic Joan of Arc who heard voices and saw visions and who made no move unless she was spiritually guided."[35] She described the Nation crowd as "the most intemperate temperance workers."[36] "Mrs. Nation is not eloquent, and expresses herself more fluently with a hatchet than by words, but she has that strong, invincible, irresistible power that comes to those who are ready to lay down their lives, if needed, for the cause they have espoused."[37] Her account of the fanatical crusade of the temperance leader won respect from *Journal* editors and readers alike.

The Hearst management recognized Dix's uncanny ability to interview people and win their confidence. The editors of the yellow press decided to capitalize on the cash potential of this ability. Though she continued writing advice columns and feature stories, they encouraged her to use her charismatic personality in other journalistic endeavors. She was assigned to cover vice investigations, political conventions, and murder trials.

In 1907 Hearst editor Arthur Brisbane assigned Dix to cover the trial of Harry K. Thaw.

NIXOLA GREELEY-SMITH

Birth to June 25, 1906

Nixola Greeley-Smith was born on April 5, 1880, at Chappaqua, New York, on the estate that her mother, Lillian (Greeley) Smith, had inherited from Nixola's grandfather, the famous editor Horace Greeley.

Greeley-Smith received her early education at Sacred Heart Convent in New York City. In the fall of 1889 her father was appointed United States consul at Three Rivers, Quebec. The family remained in Canada until February 1893 when he was reassigned as American consul at Liège, Belgium. During her two years in Belgium, Smith learned to speak fluent French, a skill that helped her immensely in future interviews with Sara Bernhardt and Marshall Foch.

Her writing career began at age twelve when she submitted a short play to the *New York World.* The piece was published, and the editor later accepted an article on the Belgium labor movement submitted on her return to America when she was sixteen years of age.[38] Joseph Pulitzer hired eighteen-year-old Greeley-Smith as a regular writer for the Sunday magazine section of the *New York World.*[39]

Her talent as an interviewer was recognized early. Though this was the height of "yellow journalism," the editor recognized her journalistic skills and did not require sensational treatment of her subjects. Her articles had a "sophisticated touch and aura of education," providing readers a pleasant change from a continuous diet of sensationalism.[40]

Greeley-Smith devoted her life to her work. She was especially successful with the personal interview. For the *Sunday World* she did a series of interviews of socially prominent women, many of whom had never before granted newspaper interviews.

The first in the series was an interview with Mrs. William Backhouse Astor, the "Queen of Society." Nixola Greeley-Smith went to her with a letter of introduction from Senator Chauncey M. Depew of New York State. Introducing Mrs. Greeley-Smith as the granddaughter of the famous publisher and journalist Horace Greeley, the senator wrote he would consider it a personal favor if Mrs. Astor would grant her an interview.[41] Senator Depew was an important figure in both New York and Washington society, and although the word "interview" was repugnant to the Queen of High Society, she could hardly deny a request from this distinguished gentleman.

When Mrs. Astor received Greeley-Smith in her drawing room, she found her to be a small, handsome women, dressed adequately but too casually to be classed as stylish. Mrs. Astor thought Greeley-Smith exuded an air of sophistication and breeding which made the "Queen" accept her as a social equal.[42]

Greeley-Smith developed a characteristic form that she used in most of her interviews. First she used an effective, attention-arousing opening. This interview began, "We have no royalty as such in America, Mrs. Astor. But what Queen Victoria is to England and the Empress Eugenie is to France, you are to the United States. People look up to you as the uncrowned Queen of Society. Your views are as important as those of the other two queens I mentioned."[43]

Mrs. Astor responded to the flattery and proceeded to give her opinion on all sorts of subjects, from politics to women's place in life. She answered Greeley-Smith's questions fully and frankly. Greeley-Smith won her completely, and before she left had an excellent interview, which Greeley-Smith promised to bring by for Mrs. Astor to read and approve before it was printed.[44]

The next day, when Greeley-Smith arrived at 840 Fifth Avenue with the article for Mrs. Astor's perusal, she was less than cordially received. Greeley-Smith waited for a long time after announcing herself to the maid. The maid reappeared with the message that Mrs. Astor was sorry that she could not see her. She held out a $2 bill and continued, "Mrs. Astor sends you this because she knows that you work for a living and that you have been put to some trouble coming here."[45]

Greeley-Smith looked at the bill and said to the maid, "Will you deliver a message exactly as I give it to you?" "Certainly," was the reply, and Greeley-Smith continued, "Tell Mrs. Astor that she not only forgets who I am, but she forgets who she is. Give her back the two dollars with my compliments, and tell her that when John Jacob Astor was skinning rabbits, my grandfather was getting out the *Tribune* and was one of the foremost citizens of New York."[46]

The paper printed the interview, the first of many that Greeley-Smith was to do with society women. The cordiality afforded

Smith by these grande dames could be attributed to her "distinguished ancestry and social position."[47] They felt it impossible to be rude to a women of "assured social grace and regal bearing."[48] She also developed a reputation of writing rather flatteringly when received graciously during an interview and with a pen dipped in vitriol when the interview was less than cordial.[49]

The series established Smith as the top woman in this specialized field of interviewing. Though essentially considered a woman's writer, in 1907 she was assigned to cover the Thaw trial for the *New York Evening World*.

ADA PATTERSON

Birth to June 25, 1906

Little is known of Ada Patterson's early life. Born in Mount Joy, Pennsylvania, in the heart of Mennonite country, it appears that her family moved to Salt Lake City shortly after her birth. At the age of fourteen she was working as a society reporter for the *Salt Lake City Herald*.[50] Patterson then moved to San Francisco where she was employed as a feature writer at the *San Francisco Call* but spent most of her time collaborating on the book *By the Stage Door*, a series of short stories published in 1902.[51]

A move to St. Louis and an article written for the *St. Louis Republican* got Patterson her first New York newspaper job. She had seen a man hanged.[52] In fact Patterson stood beside him on the scaffold while he died. The man was Dr. Arthur Duestrow, son of a St. Louis mining millionaire. One wintery day, in a drunken frenzy, the doctor, annoyed that his wife was keeping him waiting, chastised and then shot her. His child, upset at the commotion, began crying. "He seized her by the ankles and dashed out her brains against the wall."[53]

A sensational trial followed. Charles B. Johnson, former governor of Missouri, was counsel for the defense. The case was carried to the higher courts. The defense was insanity, but the verdict of guilty was affirmed. In 1897 Dr. Duestow was hanged in Union, Missouri.[54]

When the time for his execution drew near, Patterson, who was then working for the *St. Louis Republican*, was assigned to take the place of a fellow worker who was inebriated. As she had interviewed Dr. Duestrow several times in jail, her city editor thought Patterson a logical selection for the gruesome task.[55]

Patterson's colorful writing of the sensational trial that followed earned her the name of "Nellie Bly of the West."[56] Bradford Merrill, then with the *New York Evening World* and later with the *New York American*—an editor whose advertised slogan was "enterprise, vigilance and accuracy"—saw the story and summoned her to New York.[57]

When Patterson arrived in New York, Merrill was on vacation and no one working at the newspaper knew anything about a job. Short on funds and unable to crash the gates of the New York newspaper field, she was very discouraged and lamented her move east. By chance she met a man she had known in the West. He was employed at the *New York American* and encouraged Patterson to apply for a job at his paper. "Come over to our shop," he told her, "an editor wants a woman's job done in a hurry."

The editor, not one to waste words, informed Patterson that he was looking for someone to go down in the caisson of the bridge currently being built across the East River. "The men who work in the caissons," he said, "are having the bends. The air pressure is also apt to cause deafness. Want to take the risk?"[58]

Patterson bravely accepted the assignment and with it made her debut in the New York newspaper world. She wrote the story. Feeling it was an exclusive, the *American* held it out for several days. In the meantime the *World*, hearing that a woman had descended under the East River, had one of their female reporters perform the same descent. The delay resulted in the caisson story appearing simultaneously in both papers.[59]

Patterson was bitterly disappointed but realized the cut-throat nature of the newspaper business. She would not let that happen again and was first with many feature stories. She followed her ride in the caisson with a test dive in a submarine and later a ride with speeding race track drivers.[60] The exclusive stories following these experiences were always exciting, accurate, and filled with human drama.

Some of Patterson's best work was done on the trial of Nan Patterson, the Floradora girl who was charged in 1904 with murdering Caesar Young, her bookmaker lover. The public killing took place in a hansom cab. Nan Patterson was "soft-voiced and beautiful."[61] She had a patient air and was an excellent witness. Though there were witnesses who thought they saw her pull the trigger, by the time she got off the stand, the jury was convinced that Caesar Young had committed suicide.

Ada Patterson had to testify about an interview she had with the defendant in jail. Nan Patterson, struck by the similarity in their names, granted the interviews after receiving the request in a note hidden in a basket of fruit, asking for a few minutes' talk. Ada Patterson always believed Young had shot himself.

The trial proved to be sensational. Women, denied entrance because the courtroom was considered to be no place for the weaker sex, battered at the doors. By sheer force they got in and were chastised in the journals the next day.[62] Nan Patterson was acquitted and promptly faded into obscurity.

In 1907, Patterson was summoned by Arthur Brisbane, editor for the Hearst paper, to join her fellow journalist on the *New York Evening Journal*, Dorothy Dix, in covering the Thaw-White murder trial.

NOTES

1. Ishbel Ross, *Ladies of the Press*, (New York: Harper and Brothers, 1936), p. 60.

2. Ibid., p. 61.

3. John Tebbel, *The Life and Good Times of William Randolph Hearst* (New York: Hawthorne Books, 1952), p. 306.

4. Madelon Golden Schlipp and Sharon M. Murphy, *Great Women of the Press* (Carbondale, Ill.: Southern Illinois University Press, 1983), p. 149.

5. Edward T. James, ed., *Notable American Women: 1607-1950*, vol. 1 (Cambridge, Mass.: Belknap, 1971), p. 154.

6. Schlipp, *Great Women of the Press*, p. 149.

7. Ross, *Ladies of the Press*, p. 61.

8. John Jakes, *Great Women Reporters* (New York: G. P. Putnam's Sons, 1969), p. 69.

9. Ross, *Ladies of the Press*, p. 61.

10. Jakes, *Great Women Reporters*, p. 70.

11. Ibid.

12. *San Francisco Examiner*, 19 January 1890.

13. *San Francisco Examiner*, 22 January 1890.

14. Schlipp, *Great Women of the Press*, p. 150.

15. *San Francisco Examiner*, 27 February 1890.

16. *New York Times*, 26 May 1936.

17. Jakes, *Great Women Reporters*, p. 70.

18. Schlipp, *Great Women of the Press*, p. 154.

19. Ross, *Ladies of the Press*, p. 63.

20. Schlipp, *Great Women of the Press*, p. 113.

21. John E. Drewry, *Post Biographies of Famous Journalists* (Athens, Ga.: University of Georgia Press, 1942), p. 36.

22. Ibid.

23. Schlipp, *Great Women of the Press*, p. 113.

24. Drewry, *Post Biographies of Famous Journalists*, p. 36.

25. Ibid.

26. Schlipp, *Great Women of the Press*, p. 114.

27. Drewry, *Post Biographies of Famous Journalists*, p. 36.

28. Ibid.

29. Schlipp, *Great Women of the Press*, p. 114.

30. Ibid., p. 115.

31. Ross, *Ladies of the Press*, p. 78.

32. Schlipp, *Great Women of the Press*, p. 115.

33. Ibid.

34. Drewry, *Post Biographies of Famous Journalists*, p. 39.

35. Ross, *Ladies of the Press*, p. 78.

36. Schlipp, *Great Women of the Press*, p. 116.

37. Kane, *Dear Dorothy Dix*, p. 94.

38. Ross, *Ladies of the Press*, p. 93.

39. Jakes, *Great Women Reporters*, p. 84.

40. Ibid., p. 85.

41. Ross, *Ladies of the Press*, p. 86.

42. Jakes, *Great Women Reporters*, p. 78.

43. Ibid.

44. Ibid., p. 79.

45. Ross, *Ladies of the Press*, p. 87.
46. Ibid., p. 86.
47. Jakes, *Great Women Reporters*, p. 81.
48. Ibid.
49. Ibid., p. 82.
50. *New York Journal and American*, 27 June 1939.
51. Ada Patterson, *By the Stage Door* (New York: Grafton, 1902).
52. Ross, *Ladies of the Press*, p. 67.
53. Ibid., p. 68.
54. Ibid.
55. Ibid.
56. *New York Journal and American*, 27 June 1939.
57. Ross, *Ladies of the Press*, p. 68.
58. Ibid., p. 69.
59. Ibid.
60. *New York Journal and American*, 27 June 1939.
61. Ross, *Ladies of the Press*, p. 70.
62. Ibid.

Chapter 4

The Case: The Sad Butterfly

Monday, June 25, 1906, dawned hot and muggy—typical for late June in Manhattan. The *New York Times* announced that Russian spies were at the New York public libraries "keeping careful surveillance over all patrons who show a special interest in the literature of anarchy" and that sixteen automobilists were sent to prison for speeding. "Some of the automobiles," declared police, "were going as fast as thirty miles per hour." In other local news "women sobbed hysterically at Temple Kehilath Jeshrun when Rabbi S. M. Margolies referred to atrocities committed upon Jews in Russia"; the bravery of Policeman Robinson was noted for "stopping a runaway horse and saving many children from being injured." "Tall men and short men, wide men and narrow men with women who were very wide climbed aboard special trolley cars hired by the Knickerbocker Pinochle Club and rode from the Pickleville section of Brooklyn to Metropolitan Park to attend the annual Pinochle feat." "The Metropolitan Opera House Band Concert in the park was a great success playing before a larger than usual crowd which applauded every number, forcing the band to give several encores."

Elsewhere in the country "the new governor of Ohio became ill and took to his bed." His wife wished to summon a physician, but he forbade her to do so, stating that medicine would "surely make him critically ill"; "a gigantic sturgeon, the largest fish ever seen in Pittsburgh's local waters" seized a 10 year old boy and held him in his mouth until it (the fish) was killed"; "a case of yellow fever was reported at the Mississippi Quarantine Center below New Orleans"; and "Samuel Gompers of the A.F. of L. sent representatives to Chicago to arrange for a 'union exposition' to celebrate the achievements of organized labor."

On the international scene King Haakon and Queen Maud of Denmark received an American delegation congratulating the king on his ascendancy to the throne; King Alfonso of Spain and Queen Victoria of Britain were meeting aboard a royal yacht; a woman named Miss Jane Morgan was to pilot a yacht through the Mediterranean. "She knows all about taking the sun, how to figure out the latitude and longitude in which her vessel is and she can even set course after the North Star."

Advertisements in the *Times* of that day suggested that "the most impressive dignity is worn beneath a Knox hat" and that there is "no need of your looking like a damp rag in your bathing suit" when "we can give you the opportunity to get a $2.25 bathing suit for $1.50." Furthermore, a 100-piece complete porcelain dinner set could be purchased for $7.75. In addition, "to be frank—you really never have eaten a true soda cracker until you've eaten a Uneeda biscuit."[1]

The continued heat, humidity, and fumes made the evening of June 25, 1906, almost unbearable. The poor headed for the roof tops in an attempt to catch some of the harbor's sea breeze. The middle class also took to the roof tops not only to escape the heat, but because roof-gardens, restaurants, and theaters offered them an "evening of gaiety and romance."[2] The Roof Garden Theatre and Restaurant at Madison Square Garden was premiering a musical entitled *Mamzelle Champagne*, starring Maud Fulton, with book and lyrics by Edgar Allen Wolf and music by Cassius Freeborn.[3]

Mr. and Mrs. Thaw were staying in New York while waiting to board the *Amerikas* for Europe and a visit with Harry's mother, who had chosen to leave two days earlier.[4] Evelyn, still enamored of the theater, was looking forward with great anticipation to June 25, 1906, and the opening of *Mamzelle Champagne*. She wanted to see it because it was Freeborn's first musical and he would conduct it himself.[5]

The evening began at Martin's, a French cafe, on Twenty-sixth Street between Broadway and Fifth Avenue. Here they met Thomas McCaleb and Truxton Beale, two of Thaw's friends from his Pittsburgh days. "The Thaw party was near the aisle along one side of the great room. Harry Thaw, as host, sat with his back to the room, Truxton Beale sat on his left, Thomas McCaleb on his right, and Evelyn sat opposite Harry, where she could watch the room and the parade of diners."[6]

During dinner they chatted freely. In the midst of Evelyn's conversation, Harry noticed a change in her. When Harry tried to discern the problem, she "wrote a note, folded the paper, and passed it across the table. The note read: 'That B is here'."[7]

After receiving the note, Harry found further conversation at the Thaw table impossible. He began to stare and bite his fingernails. Evelyn feared that he would start a scene and encouraged him to pay the check, so that they might depart for the theater.

On the balcony Stanford White dined with his eighteen-year-old son, Lawrence Grant White, and Lawrence's Harvard classmate, LeRoy King. After dinner the boys had gotten tickets to see a performance of George M. Cohan's new review, *The Governor's Son*, at the New York Theatre Roof Garden. Stanford White drove them to the theater in a hansom cab and then went to Madison Square Garden.[8]

Tall, with shocking red hair and a bristling mustache, strong, enthusiastic, vigorous and versatile, always in a hurry, always talking, Stanford White was just the man to become the leader of a restless generation. Born in New York City on November 9, 1853, Stanford White was a member of a family that had been established in this country for over 220 years.[9] From his earliest youth, while living in an old colonial frame house at Fort Hamilton on the Narrows in Brooklyn, Stanford White wanted to be a painter.[10] However, following consultation with John LaFarge, the world's acknowledged master in work in stained glass, Stanford was encouraged to try architecture. Unfortunately, there were no architecture schools in America.

In 1872, he moved to Boston and became an apprentice to Harry Hobson Richardson, one of the few trained architects in America and considered by most to be a genius. In Richardson's office White met and worked with Charles Fallem McKim, also an architect with H. H. Richardson and a graduate of the Beaux Arts in Paris.

In late 1879, White accepted a position with Charles McKim, and the firm McKim, Mead and White was born. The three differed: "McKim, the calm and deliberate scholar, the academician, something of a pedant in his insistence upon historic truth; White, the enthusiast, the firebrand, impatient of schools and formulas; Mead, the engineer."[11] It has been said that White's buildings greet you informally, invite you in; whereas McKim's "seem to command, bidding you 'Halt and kneel if need be'."[12] Mead was both rudder and anchor. His common sense steered the firm through many difficulties.

McKim, Mead and White were artists and never allowed themselves to become commercialized. Clients and money were plentiful. The partnership was an extraordinary success from its inception. The talent of each partner was complemented by the others, and they combined their talents in superb collaboration. "To White, an artist, architecture meant color first, and form and texture next, and proportion afterward, and plan last of all. To handle material fitly, to adjust it to a new use, to devise its characteristic detail, to combine it with others consummately, to employ all that is beautiful in the old with all that is practical in the new—these things were a constant pleasure to him."[13]

Stanford began to practice—and preach—Italian Renaissance as a style and a tradition better suited to American needs than any or all phases of Gothic, Romanesque, or Classic architecture.[14] He felt that "our modern social intellectual life dated from the Renaissance, an age that could be imitative without sacrifice of its own individuality, and daringly original without losing touch with the corrective and living traditions of the past."[15]

In its heyday the firm of McKim, Mead and White was responsible for the design and implementation of such famous landmarks as the Boston Public Library, the Triumphal Arch on Washington Square in New York City, honoring our first president, and Madison Square Garden. Completed in 1890, Madison Square Garden, Stanford White's "Palace of Pleasures," has been described as a series of "loggias, riches, girandoles, cartouches, carved flora and fauna, columned belvederes, shielded colonnade, and ornate flourishes."[16] White would explain that he "was concerned not only with the design and form of the building itself but how it would look, how it would feel, when the cigarette smoke curled up into the yellow spotlights—how the color would sound when the band struck-up, how the arena would smell when the scents of powder and perfume and the acrid odors of excitement were mixed."[17] Opening night, June 16, 1890, was heralded by the *New York Times* as "one of the most brilliant ever witnessed." It was agreed that this was a landmark to equal the Statue of Liberty, the Brooklyn Bridge, and Central Park.

In his role as man-about-town, Stanford White was constantly searching for new and interesting people. This search took him off Fifth Avenue and over to Broadway. He became a familiar figure both "before and behind the footlights."[18] His taste for the stage was all on the light side, predominantly music shows, though he sometimes "endured to sit through a tragedy."[19] There were plenty of girl-and-music shows that were worth attending.

It was while attending a performance of *Floradora* that White met Evelyn Nesbit, a member of the dance company. Evelyn Florence Nesbit was born on Christmas Day 1884 in the town of Tarentum about twenty-four miles up the Allegheny River from Pittsburgh. Her father, Winfield Scott Nesbit, a successful Philadelphia lawyer and famous amateur bicycle racer,[20] died when Evelyn was eight years old.[21] That event changed the course of life for Evelyn, her mother, and brother Howard, two years and two months younger.

They moved to another house where Evelyn's mother tried her best to eke out a living by letting rooms. Though never "rich," the Nesbits had lived well in Tarentum, and Evelyn found poverty "annoying" because she was not accustomed to it.[22] Running a series of boarding houses, Evelyn's mother cooked, washed, ironed, and cleaned rooms for boarders to make ends meet. But she was not the type to be a successful boarding-house keeper, since she had always been a sheltered, protected, married woman. Eventually, she was forced to sell off their furniture and possessions in order to keep the family fed and clothed. Days with scarcely anything to eat were becoming commonplace. In desperation, Evelyn's mother decided to leave Pittsburgh for Philadelphia, a big city where she might get a chance as a dress designer, but lack of experience kept Mrs. Nesbit from realizing such a position. Instead, all three family members secured jobs as sales clerks at Wanamaker's, a large, fashionable Philadelphia department store. Schooldays over, Evelyn, at fourteen, was a working girl.

A friend, thinking Evelyn extraordinarily beautiful, introduced her to Violet Oakley, designer of stained-glass windows for churches, who promptly engaged her as a model. At fourteen, almost fifteen, Evelyn began to pose for other artists including George Gibbs and Niels Thompson, illustrators of books, magazines, and stories. Artists raved over her beauty. Her deep eyes, described as the colors of blue-brown pansies, had long upper lids which kept them obscured most of the time. Her eyebrows arched gently to frame her eyes. Her long hair was copper color and worn in a mass of curls surrounding the oval of her face and creating a contrast for her eyes. Her face, perfectly contoured, was long and narrow with a pointed chin. Irwin S. Cobb described Evelyn as having "the slim, quick grace of a fawn, a head that sat on a flawless throat as a lily on its stem, eyes that were the size of half-dollars, and a mouth made of rumpled rose petals."[23]

Artists saw a dewy innocence of childhood that breathed from every feature. Moreover, she was plastic. She could assume any position, any expression, portray any emotion, and she became an ideal model.[24] Evelyn soon had more work than she could handle. Among those for whom she posed were George Grey Bernard, the sculptor, who used her for his famous study "Innocence," later on view at the Metropolitan Museum of Arts; and Charles Dana Gibson, for whom she posed in the pen and ink sketch of "The Eternal Question."[25] Newspapers, including the *New York Sunday World* and the *New York Sunday Journal*, devoted full-page stories to her, touting her as the new artists' ideal of feminine beauty.

Lured by the newspaper stories, a Broadway theatrical producer arranged a meeting for Evelyn with impresarios responsible for the musical *Floradora.*[26] In 1901 Broadway witnessed Evelyn Nesbit's debut as a member of the sextette of the Floradora Company. During a matinee shortly after joining the company, Evelyn was introduced to Stanford White.

Their first social evening was spent in his house on West Twenty-fourth Street. Here Evelyn saw for the first time the red velvet swing, later popularized by a movie of the same name. It was also in this house that Evelyn awoke on a bed in the "Mirror Room," clad only in an abbreviated pink undergarment, with Stanford White lying beside her. On this occasion Stanford White proclaimed her to be his.

Evelyn's intimate relationship with White continued until Harry K. Thaw, scion to coalmining fortunes, entered her life. The son of William Thaw and Mary Sibbet (Copley) Thaw was born on February 1, 1871. William Thaw, a high official in the Pennsylvania Company, had amassed a fortune in coalmine leases, franchises in railroad feeder lines from "minebend to hearthpit," and related enterprises.

The Thaw family, including ten children, was among Pittsburgh's most prominent. They lived at Lyndhurst, a mansion built in 1888 at an estimated cost of $2.5 million. They were intimates of the Carnegies, Fricks, and Mellons, and they provided generous endowments of art and education as well as scholarships in science at Harvard and Princeton.[27]

In 1889 William Thaw died. His will clearly expressed his father's opinion of Harry as an idler: "with great regret and reluctance and solely from a sense of duty, I hereby cancel and revoke any and all provisions of my said will directing payment of money or property to my said son, Harry Kendall Thaw."[28]

Instead of passing along as an inheritance, his money was to be managed by a trust fund "for his maintenance during his minority."[29] Mrs. Thaw, saddened by her husband's treatment of Harry, used her authority as executrix of Harry's trust fund to provide him with an allowance of $80,000 a year.[30] Dorothy Dix claimed:

> Thaw spent his days in riotous living, in mad escapades that were the talk of two continents, knowing no law but his own will, no restraints, no self-control, utterly and entirely an egotist who lived for his own pleasure and believed that there was nothing he could not do and pay for with a check.[31]

Thaw liked associating with actresses. He began to spend a lot of time at the theater, enjoying the company of the talented dancers in the *Floradora* sextette. Although Evelyn took no notice of him, he made overtures toward her, first timid approaches, then bolder ones. He began sending her American beauty roses and white gardenias, some with fifty-dollar bills wrapped around the stems.[32]

His persistence paid off, and Evelyn succumbed to the amorous attentions of this wealthy bachelor nicknamed "Johnny." Their relationship at first involved only occasional dinners at New York's most exclusive dining establishments, but it soon intensified. In May 1903, after convincing Evelyn's mother that her daughter was in great need of rest, the three sailed aboard the *S. S. New York* for England.

During this trip, which included dining, theater going, clothes shopping, and meeting the rich and famous of Europe, Evelyn first observed Thaw's idiosyncrasies, erratic behavior, fits of temper, and sadistic inclinations. She described this revelation in *Prodigal Days*:

> In one swift, violent jerk he stripped me. Horror-stricken, a gurgling scream escaped my lips. He clapped his hand over my mouth.

The look on his face at that moment I shall never forget! His eyes were glassy, the pupils enormously dilated. His face was livid like a death-mask—the lips drawn into a thin, cruel line.

"Keep quiet!" he breathed. "Keep quiet!" and then he raised his right arm. In his hand he clutched a dog-whip. Suddenly it descended, and a thin stream of fire seemed to singe my flesh.

The beating continued, blood streaming from the lacerations until it ceased as suddenly as it had begun. The demon in Thaw died out. His eyes changed remarkably; all the glassiness and glare had gone out of them.[33]

Notwithstanding the humiliation and beatings Evelyn experienced, she chose to believe Thaw's proclamations of remorse and reformation. Evelyn Nesbit married Harry K. Thaw on April 5, 1905.[34]

The Thaws' arrival at the Madison Square Garden Roof Top Theatre was noticed by fellow theater goers, not only because of Harry Thaw's notoriety but because, despite an outdoor temperature just over eighty degrees, Thaw was wearing a long black coat over his dinner jacket. Shortly after their arrival, Thaw wandered off, moving about the tables and speaking with people. He continued visiting through most of the performance.

Engrossed in the finale, White did not notice that Thaw had made his way along the aisle to within "three feet of White's table."[35] "From beneath his black overcoat Thaw pulled out a revolver, held it at arm's length, and as White felt his presence and turned toward him, Thaw aimed for the eyes, then fired three shots."[36]

White's elbow slid from the table, taking the edge of the tablecloth, and in the sudden silence silverware scattered and a wine glass crashed.[37]

Harry Thaw held the pistol over his head to signal the end of the shooting. He emptied the revolver chambers and walked toward the elevators where he was placed under arrest by Officer Debes of the Tenderloin District Command.[38] The Tenderloin District was named in 1876 by Police Captain Alexander S. Williams, who, upon his transfer to the district, claimed he had had nothing but rump steak for a long time and now he was going to get a little tenderloin. The figure of speech referred to a suggestion of blackmail and graft. It was a section of theaters, plush brothels, and noisy dance halls, wide open to lawlessness and considered a kind of "safety valve necessary in an era of repression and prudery."[39]

After the shooting Evelyn reached her husband. Throwing her arms around his neck she asked, "Oh, Harry, why did you do it?" Hugging her, he was overheard saying, "It's all right dear. It's all right. I have probably saved your life."[40]

Following the shooting Thaw was driven rapidly to police headquarters, taken first into Inspector McLaughlin's office, and then led upstairs into the Rogue's Gallery, where he was measured and photographed. He was sent from Police Headquarters to the Jefferson Market Police Court, where he was arraigned on a charge of homicide and remanded to the custody of the coroner.[41] He was next taken to the Tombs and assigned a cell on murderers' row to await the action of the grand jury.[42]

After the pronouncement Thaw asked to use the phone and called Anthony Comstock, president of the Society for the Suppression of Vice. This was not Comstock's first contact with Thaw. In February 1903, Thaw called Comstock with information about "three dens White maintained," claiming that White had "ravished three hundred and seventy eight innocent American girls."[43] Comstock accepted Thaw's testimony and promised he would investigate the matter. This was the last contact the two gentlemen had until after the murder. Following Thaw's call, Comstock talked with reporters, claiming he had information to present to the grand jury that was damaging to Stanford White. This was the beginning of an unparalleled slander campaign.

Ella Wheeler Wilcox in the June 30, 1906, edition of the *New York Journal* wrote:

When the best industrial interests of the island of Jamaica were jeopardized by an animal which insinuated itself into the heart of young fruit and destroyed it before it matured, the Government sent to East India and imported the mongoose. Not only did the mongoose kill the fruit enemy, but he also exterminated the cobra and other poisonous reptiles from Jamaica.

She then went on to call Harry Thaw the "human mongoose." "He killed," she wrote, "to rid the earth of dangerous animals; reptiles more poisonous than the deadly cobra, and creatures more destructive to the future of America than any four-footed beast or scaly serpent known to the jungle or the zoo." Wilcox went on:

White indulged to excess those appetites which God gave man to indulge in moderation. He excited his blood by unnatural stimulants and overspiced foods, and he allowed his artistic and voluptuous imagination full license and looked with envy upon every woman who possessed beauty or charm. Whether such men dwell in the slums or in haunts of fashion and wealth, they are equally depraved, and when swift and sudden vengeance fall on them, the least of all their crimes has been added to their list; they have created their own "executioners," and the beginning of their punishment is violent and shameful death. After death comes realization and remorse.[44]

Arrangements had been made by Charles B. McKim for Stanford White to be buried on Thursday, June 28, 1906, in a little cemetery adjoining Saint Bartholomew's Episcopal Church in the town of St. James on Long Island.[45] Only five persons followed the body of Stanford White from his residence at 121 East Twenty-first Street to the Long Island Railroad depot. They were Mrs. White, Lawrence White, the son, Peter Cooper Hewitt, and one of Mrs. White's sisters with her husband. Others went directly to the railroad station and boarded the pullman awaiting them there.[46]

The first trial of the *State of New York vs. Harry Kendall Thaw* was scheduled in the Criminal Branch of the Supreme Court of New York for January 23, 1907, six months after he entered the Tombs. Dorothy Dix commented:

> Today the wheels of justice—ponderous, slow, solemn, majestic, turned once again, and the mighty machinery of the law begin grinding out the destiny of Harry Thaw, who on the twenty-fifth day of last June slew Stanford White, on the Madison Square Roof Garden.
>
> No murder case in a century has been so much written about, so much theorized about, so much talked about as this one. From the beginning it has been a foreordained *cause celebre*, not only because of the spectacular and dramatic method of the killing, but because every one connected with it to the remotest degree belonged to that little group in this country who keep themselves always in the spot light of publicity, and concerning whose doings, their comings and their goings, their amusements, their clothes, every detail of life, is of inexhaustible curiosity.[47]

The *New York Times* on that date stated, "The Thaw trial is being reported to the ends of the civilized globe. Due to the eminence of the victim, the wealth of the prisoner, the dramatic circumstances of the crime, and the light it sheds not only on Broadway life, but on the doings of the fast set in every capital."[48] Indeed a telegraph office had been set up in the main hall of the building; wires were hanging from a central skylight.

Prominently seated at a special table in the front of the court room were four female reporters chosen by their prestigious newspapers to cover the trial: Winifred Black, Dorothy Dix, Nixola Greeley-Smith, and Ada Patterson. Other journalists, either not as lucky or not as influential, were seated in another section of the courtroom known as the "royal pew." Here sat Irwin Cobb, reporting the trial for the *New York Evening World*. As soon as he began to read the copy produced by the four "chosen" press women, he dubbed them the "sob sisters," a name chosen to describe their sentimental reportage.[49]

Since the courtroom was likely to be filled to capacity with reporters, lawyers, and witnesses, extra seats were added. Just after ten o'clock the Thaw women filed in. Mrs. William Thaw, the defendant's mother, entered first, her costume of "unrelieved black" offset only by her white hair. She was followed by her daughters, the Countess of Yarmouth ("a pretty young woman with a tip-tilted nose") and Mrs. George Lauder Carnegie ("a plainer type"). Then came Evelyn Nesbit, her complexion pale by fright or by design, "looking almost shabby" in a black coat and white veil. As if for comic relief, Nesbit was followed by her friend from the Floradora days, May McKenzie, dressed in a brilliant purple suit and sporting a gaudy hat from which "trailed two long feathers." The five women were followed anticlimactically by Harry's brother Edward and brother-in-law George Carnegie.[50]

Shortly thereafter the six defense lawyers took their places around their table: Clifford Hartridge, (the family lawyer and personal friend), Daniel O'Reilly, John B. Gleason, George Peabody, Hugh McMink, and their leader Delphin Michael Delmas. "How he [Delmas] chanced to be named 'the Napoleon of the Western Bar' was at once apparent for he marvelously resembled the portraits of the Emperor of France. Short of stature, with an oversized leonine head and heavy pouches under his eyes and jaws, Delmas conducted himself with imperial dignity."[51]

Suddenly the court clerk announced "All rise" and the trial of the *People of New York State vs. Harry Kendall Thaw* opened. The corpulent judge, James Fitzgerald, was seated and a hushed atmosphere overtook the courtroom as the spectators took their seats. District Attorney William Travers Jerome read the indictment, and Harry Kendall Thaw was beckoned to the bar.[52] Nixola Greeley-Smith described the moment:

Four hundred heads turned to the door. Its opening meant the beginning of the great trial.

There was a dramatic pause—a breathless moment of suspense timed as effectively as if we had been witnessing a mimic drama instead of the closing scenes of a real life tragedy of love and sin, and smoldering hatred and sudden death.

Then Harry Thaw came in, and, apparently oblivious of the straining focus of so many eyes upon him, walked with a sidewise, shoulder-first motion toward the table at which he is to sit throughout the trial with his counsel, and sat down. His face was white, his weak jaw set rigidly. He did not look toward the line of faithful women who since 10 o'clock had sat patiently waiting for him—though the eyes of mother, sisters, and wife yearned toward him.[53]

Jury selection was to begin. When Judge Fitzgerald announced that for the first time in the history of murder trials the jury would be sequestered for the length of the trial, it became apparent that it would take a good while for the jury to be selected.[54] In addition to the usual weeding out of potential jurors, "the number of certified excuses multiplied geometrically, and the number of veniremen who claimed to have known the dead architect suddenly soared. The selection of twelve good men and true slowed to a snail's pace."[55] The first question asked of every juror was "Have you any conscientious scruples that would prevent your bringing in a verdict of death should you be convinced beyond all reasonable doubt of the guilt of the accused?"[56]

Jury selection was long and tedious. On Friday, February 1, 1907, ten days after *voir dire* began, the twelfth juror was selected, and both sides agreed to allow the jury to stand as chosen. "On account of the importance of the case and the strenuous efforts being made to influence public opinion, the twelve jurors selected were to be housed and fed on the Broadway Central Hotel and allowed to see their families only in the presence of a guard."[57] So ended the preparations for the trial and so began the unique press coverage by the four "sob sisters."

The tedium and suspense of the opening days had a visible effect on Evelyn. Nixola Greeley-Smith wrote: "She alone of Thaw's relatives seems unable to accustom herself to her strange surroundings. One observes the added pallor and weariness of her wraithlike face, gleaming under the folds of the blue veil she had resumed wearing."[58] Dorothy Dix, pulling at the heartstrings of the readership, says of Evelyn:

> In good truth, a more piteous figure than the little chorus girl and artists' model could scarcely be imagined. Gone was even the bravado of cheerfulness and nonchalance she had been trying so vainly to keep up for the past two days. She came into court looking like a flower that has been beaten down into the ground and despoiled of its beauty by a storm. Her face was sodden with weeping. Her eyes red rimmed and swollen. Her face showed white and wan under the black veil in which she had tried to shroud it. She had seemed sad and miserable before. She appeared absolutely crushed, and as if there was no spirit left in her.[59]

Ada Patterson wrote:

> The Three Fates—the Spinner, the Measurer, and the Severer—looked over the Judge's ample shoulders, past the heads of the jurymen, upon an unexpected sight yesterday. They saw the semi-collapse of the brave little wife of the prisoner.[60]

Testimony began on Monday, February 4, 1907, with a brief statement by Assistant District Attorney Garvan. Thaw's shooting of White, stated Garvan, "was a cool, deliberate, malicious, premeditated murder, and we shall ask for a verdict of murder in the first degree."[61]

The first day of deliberations proved to be an unfortunate example of legal ineptitude on the part of the defense. John B.

Gleason led the defense legal staff. He was not a courtroom lawyer and had never pleaded a criminal case.[62] Dorothy Dix assessed Gleason as "a successful civil lawyer, but one who lacks all of the qualities—quickness of perception, clearness of thought, directness of speech and personal magnetism that go to make up a fine criminal lawyer."[63] They wandered from place to place in an attempt both to discredit the unwritten law and to hold on to it. By the end of the day it was unanimously decided that Gleason was to be replaced by Delphin Michael Delmas as chief of the defense staff. The duel between Delmas and District Attorney Jerome was to begin.

On the second day, Evelyn Thaw was called to the stand by the attorney for the defense. Dressed in a plain navy blue suit with a shirtwaist and a schoolboy's stiff collar tied with a black bow she looked "tiny and helpless" as a grieved child. Dorothy Dix expressed the sentiments of most when she wrote:

> Once she was the gay little butterfly of the studio and the chorus, dancing down every wind of pleasure, blown hither and thither at a breath of caprice or desire. Now the butterfly has found a soul. Somewhere in the night it was born, and today she looks out upon the world with new eyes and new purposes.
>
> No nun could have kept herself more secluded from the world than has she, since her husband killed Stanford White. That night for her the old life of pleasure ended as if cloister walls had closed in about her. She who had loved the glitter and the glare of cafe life has eaten her lonely meals in her own apartments. She who adored the theatre has not seen a play this winter. She who pined for gay company and laughter has had no companions save her own dark thoughts, except an occasional woman caller.[64]

Throughout her testimony Evelyn's relationship with White was not admissible as evidence, but anything she had told Thaw concerning her past was acceptable because of its possible influence on Thaw's mental condition before the murder. Instructing the jury of that fact, Judge Fitzgerald asked Delmas to begin questioning. Delmas called Evelyn to the stand. She entered the room wearing the same costume she had worn since the first day of the trial and would continue to wear until the last—a plain navy blue suit, with shirtwaist, and a schoolboy's stiff collar tied with a black bow.[65] There was a palpable expectancy in the air when he asked his first question. No one was disappointed. His voice was beautiful, deep, and sonorous, with the timbre of a fine violin. He spoke slowly, impressively, with a little flourish of courtesy that made you think of minuets and ruffles and satin breeches.[66] His questions were incisive and aimed at gathering statistical information.

Q. At the time Mr. Thaw proposed to you, at that time did you accept his offer or did you refuse it?

A. I refused it.

Q. Did you state to him the reasons you refused it?

A. I did.

Q. Were those reasons based on any event in your life?

A. They were. . . .

Q. In stating the reasons to Mr. Thaw why you refused his offer, did you state a reason to him that was based on an event in your life with which Stanford White was connected?

A. I did.

Q. Then will you kindly give us the whole of that conversation from beginning to end?

A. He told me again he loved me, and he always would take care of me, he always would see no harm ever came to me, and he wouldn't think any less of me if I told it, and he wanted me to tell it. So I began by telling him how and where I had first met Stanford White.

Q. Then will you kindly repeat it to the jury. What you told him of your first meeting with Stanford White, and what followed if anything?

Evelyn went on to describe the first meeting with Stanford White as she had told it to Thaw.

I received a note from Mr. White at the theatre asking me to come to a party and he would send a carriage for me. So after the theatre I got into the carriage and was taken down to the Twenty-fourth Street studio, and when I got there the door opened and I went upstairs and Mr. White was there, but no one else was there, and I asked him if the other people would be at the party. And he said, "What do you think? They have turned us down." And I said, "Oh it's too bad. Then we won't have a party." He said, "They have turned us down and probably gone off somewhere else and forgotten all about us." And I said, "Had I better go home?" And he said, "No, we will sit down and have some food anyhow, in spite of them," that I must be hungry. So we sat down at the table, and I took off my hat and coat.

We sat down at the table and ate the food. Then I remember Mr. White going away for a while and coming back. So after the supper, when I got up from the table, he told me that I hadn't seen all of his place, that they had three floors and there were some very beautiful things in all the different rooms and he would take me around and show them to me. So we went up another flight of stairs, not the one I had gone up before, but a little tiny back stairs, and came into a strange room that I hadn't seen before, and there was a piano in the room, paintings on the wall and very interesting cabinets all about, and we looked at this room for some time, and I sat down at the piano and played something.

Mr. White asked me to come to see the back room and he went through some curtains, and the back room was a bedroom, and I sat down at the table, a tiny little table. There was a bottle of champagne, a small bottle and one glass. Mr. White picked up the bottle and poured the glass full of champagne. I paid no attention to him, because I was looking at a picture over the mantle, a very beautiful one that attracted my attention. Then he told me he had decorated this room by himself, and showed me all the different things about it. It was very small. Then he came to me and told me to finish my champagne, which I did, and I don't know whether it was a minute after or two minutes after, but a pounding began in my ears, then the whole room seemed to go around. Everything got very flat.

Evelyn was obviously distressed by the memory of the evening. Her face became contracted, with a strained agonized expression in her eyes. She nervously clasped and unclasped her hands and cried. Mr. Delmas sympathetically coaxed her to continue her testimony.

Then, I woke up, all my clothes were pulled off of me, and I was in bed. I sat up in the bed, and started to scream. Mr. White was there and got up and put on one of the kimonos. The kimono was lying on a chair, and then I moved up and pulled some covers over me and there were mirrors all around the bed. There were mirrors on the side of the wall and on top. Then I screamed, and he came over and asked me to please keep quiet, that I must not make so much noise. He said, "It is all over, it is all over." Then I screamed, "Oh, no!" And then he brought a kimono over to me and he went out of the room. Then as I got out of the bed I began to scream more than ever. Then he came back into the room and tried to quiet me. I don't remember how I got my clothes on or how I went home, but he took me home. Then he went away and left me, and I sat up all night.

Q. Where was Mr. White, madam, at the time you regained your conscious-ness? You say you found that you had been stripped. Did you describe to Mr. Thaw where White was?

A. Yes. He was right there beside me.

Q. Where?

A. In the bed.

Q. Dressed or undressed?

A. Completely undressed.

Q. Did you tell anything more on that occasion to Mr. Thaw than what you
   have related?

A. I told him Mr. White came to me again—I was sitting there in the chair. I
   had not eaten anything and I had not gone to bed. . . . He told me that I must
   not be worried about what had occurred. He said that everything was all
   right. He said he thought I had the most beautiful hair he had ever seen. He
   said he would do a great many things for me. He said everybody did these
   things; that all people were doing those things, that that is all people were
   for, all they lived for. He said that I was so nice and young and slim, that
   he couldn't help it and so did it.

Evelyn stopped then, wrung her hands and hesitated before
proceeding.

Then he told me that only very young girls were nice, and the
thinner they were, the prettier they were; and that nothing was
so loathsome as fat, and that I must never get fat. And then I
looked at him and said, "Does everybody you know do these
things?" And he said, "Yes." And the first thing I could think
of was the *Floradora Sextette*. I asked him if the sextette did
these things. He sat down and started to laugh, and he laughed
and laughed and laughed. Then he said, "That is a good
thing."

Then I asked him did several other people that I had met
do these things, and he said, "They all do." He said everybody
did these things, that is all people live for. He said the great
thing in this world was not to be found out, that I must be very
clever about it. He made me swear that I would not tell my
mother, not to say one word to mother about it, that I must
not tell anyone about it. That people did not talk about these
things, and did not tell about them. He said that some girls at
the theatre were very foolish and got talked about. He said
they ought to see how the society women understood and how
they realized that the great thing in this world was not to get
found out. He spoke of several who were very clever about
it. . . .

Nixola Greeley-Smith was deeply moved by the questioning on February 7, and gushed in her column:

> There is a legend, immortalized by Tennyson, of Godiva, wife of the Lord of Coventry, who rode naked through the town to save her people from starvation. There was a drama of Maeterlinck's which tells us how Monna Vanna, virtuous wife of Guldo, went clad only in a cloak to Prinzivalle's tent to ransom her besieged city of Pisa.
>
> Godiva rode, "clothed only with chastity." Monna Vanna entered Prinzivalle's tent wrapped in the same protecting innocence.
>
> Stripping herself of even this cloak, baring her inmost soul of its last garment of reserve before hundreds of alien eyes, Evelyn Nesbit Thaw has laid down everything that womanhood holds precious to save her husband, Harry Thaw.
>
> If her story, told yesterday in Justice Fitzgerald's court, had come to us in the guise of a wonderful poem or a great novel, we would realize that her sacrifice was greater than either of these fabled heroines. Because its being was a courtroom and its incentive a trial for murder, we may not be able to do justice to this marvelous story—the greatest ever told in the annals of American justice.
>
> You know already the story of this pale child, the frightened chronicle of the horrible wrong she suffered at the hands of Stanford White which drove Harry Thaw to madness and sent White to death.
>
> The story was told clearly, simply, by a girl of twenty-two who looked like a child of eleven—not like a woman who in that brief time has known the deepest sorrow and the blackest shame.
>
> The girl weighed possibly one hundred pounds, though probably not so much. The thinness of her figure was concealed by the straight lines of the loose, blue tailored suit she has worn from the beginning of the trial. She wears her brown hair parted and drawn softly back from her white forehead.

Her eyes are large and brown and very soft. There is no look of passion or experience in them, no record of the dark scenes they have innocently inspired and tragically looked upon. Her face has the pallor of the camellia blossom, to which she has been so frequently and aptly compared.

Her body sways forward as she talks as a lily broken on its stalk. Her mouth alone affords a key to the loves she has inspired. It is a full mouth, with ripe, curving lips that close over her slightly pointed teeth with difficulty.

The voice that issues from it is cold and crystalline as a forest spring. It has not very many tones in it, and might, if heard too often, seem monotonously sweet. The English it gives utterance to is extremely good. It broke only once that was when she told the frightful experience of her meeting at Stanford White's studio and spoke of their effects on Harry Thaw to whom she reiterated them.

"He sobbed and sobbed," she said, and then a sob came in her own slim white throat, her pale face twitched and one or two tears forced their way past her lowered lids.

When Mr. Delmas, in his gentlest voice, asked her to tell the jury what was the final explanation of the childish "Just be-cause!" with which she had refused to marry Thaw, she swallowed once or twice before she was able to speak. But, when the story was begun she told it bravely to the end, and at the end she was the most self-possessed woman in Justice Fitzgerald's court; and there were many men present who seemed to have their feelings under less control.[67]

Mr. Delmas continued questioning the witness.

Q. Did you state anything to Mr. Thaw on that occasion other than you have stated?
A. I don't remember anything more. . . .
Q. What was the effect of this statement of yours upon Mr. Thaw?
A. He became very excited.
Q. Will you kindly describe it?

A. He would get up and walk up and down the room a minute and then come and sit down and say, "Oh, God! Oh, God!" and bite his nails like that and keep sobbing.

Q. Sobbing?

A. Yes, it was not like crying. It was a deep sob. He kept saying "Go on, go on, tell me the whole thing about it."

Q. After you had stated this occurrence, madam, and the reason why you could not accept Mr. Thaw's offer in marriage, did he renew his offer or break it off?

A. Not that night. But that night he told me that any decent person who heard that story would say it was not my fault. That whatever happened was not my fault. That I was simply a poor, unfortunate little girl, and that he did not think anything less of me. But on the contrary, he said that I must always remember he would be my friend, and no matter what happened, he would always be my friend.

Q. When was it after that he renewed his proposal of marriage, if at all to you?

A. He kept saying he could not care for anybody else and could not possibly love anybody else; that his whole life was ruined; he could not marry anybody, and he said he never would marry anybody else.

Ada Patterson reported this testimony in what came to be typical "sob sister" fashion.

After the tragedy of her betrayed childhood which Evelyn Nesbit Thaw revealed the first day on the witness stand, all that followed, no matter how dark and sorrowful, was bound to come as a kind of anti-climax.

The worst had been told. Nothing else could ever approach the horror of that story of a poor, beautiful, foolish, ignorant girl of sixteen pursued with the wealth and ferocity of a panther, by a man old enough to be her grandfather. How he marked her for his prey when he first saw her, a slim young child dancing on the stage; how he stalked her down; how he wooed her to him with gifts; how he lulled her suspicions to rest, and how, when she utterly trusted him and revered him like a god for what she thought was his goodness to her, he turned upon her and slayed all that was pure and innocent in her, made up a recital that seemed to those who heard it to drip blood at every word.

So yesterday, when she went back upon the witness stand, her testimony, sad enough and black enough as it was, heaven knows, lacked something of the poignancy of the day before. But if the first day she had drawn the outlines of the picture, yesterday she filled in the details, and showed how Stanford White, not content with having robbed her of her good name, schemed to separate her from the only man who had ever offered her an honest love in all her toy-life, and planned to make her the lowest of all created things—a woman black-mailer.

Two figures stand out prominently in the picture, one of Stanford White, always seeking to drag the girl down, the other, Harry Thaw, always trying to save her, to protect her, to try to lift her up. As the trial progresses, one strange thing becomes more and more apparent, and that is that of the mire in which all the personages concerned in this case were sunk, there bloomed one white flower of purity and goodness, as a lily might spring from a muck heap, and that was Harry Thaw's love for Evelyn Nesbit.

No matter what he may have been. No matter if he was waster, spendthrift, debauchee as he is said to have been, he loved this woman with all that was good, honorable and chivalrous. Somewhere his affection for her struck down its roots in his heart until it came to where the eternal fountains flow, and he gives to her a love that baptizes and redeems them both. It is a love so vast that it covers her past with a mantle of forgiveness, so protecting that it seeks to shield her even from herself, so tender and comprehending that it might be love of a mother brooding over her babe.[68]

To change his line of questions, Delmas turned to Evelyn's earlier life. She described the difficulties her family encountered following the death of her father. She told about the time "the sheriff came and put a sign on the door that all the furniture was to be sold" and how her mother tried to get a position as a dress designer. "She kept failing all the time, and we lived in a little back room on the second floor, and things got very bad indeed. We didn't have anything to eat sometime for days but bread—sometimes some coffee." Fortunate to obtain employment as a photographer's model, her earnings averaged only eighteen dollars a week, she testified, which was the family's total income until she went onto the stage.

Evelyn next told the jury about her first meeting with Thaw and her trip to Europe following an appendectomy, paid for by Thaw and chaperoned by her mother. It was on this voyage that Evelyn confessed her relationship with Stanford White.

Delmas, in an attempt to illustrate the effect on the defendant's mind of Evelyn's confession, read into the record the letter Thaw had written from Europe to his lawyer, Frederick W. Longfellow, in October 1903, hoping to establish the writer's mental condition at the time.

Dear Longfellow—Mrs. Nesbit sails tomorrow for New York. She thinks I kidnapped her seventeen and three-quarter-year-old daughter. . . .

Her daughter can't be with her because Mrs. N. by super-human negligence was beguiled by a blackguard when the child was fifteen and two-thirds. The child drugged. With perfect silliness the mother was the cause and continued horrible. . . .

Telephone Mrs. N. not with your name. Say, "Did you see Mr. Thaw aboard?" After hearing answer put up phone. Finis.

H. K. T.[69]

Nixola Greeley-Smith concerned herself with the plight of Harry K. Thaw in this tragedy. She mawkishly wrote in the *Evening World* on February 8, 1907:

For two days the defendant in the Thaw case has been forgotten—the plight of Harry K. Thaw is overshadowed by the more terrible tragedy of the girl Evelyn who bared her soul to save him. In all our pity for the wife, have we realized the ordeal of the husband? Do we feel fully what it must be for the man who was fired to murder by Evelyn Thaw's story to sit passively in court and hear it retold?

More than once during that terrible recital it seemed to me that the man who heard it with staring eyes and writhing lips was about to leap to his feet and, forgetful of his fate that hung upon the narrative, force the pale, resolute girl who told it to desist. More than once I thought that but for the interposition of his lawyers, Thaw would make some demonstration in the court-room.

Perhaps only the consciousness that any outburst would be regarded as deliberately planned for its effect on the jury restrained him. There were those in court, who said of Evelyn Thaw's confession that it was a fine piece of acting—and no emotion may be so genuine that cynics will not be found to question it!

Have you ever seen Bernhardt in "La Tosca"? At any rate, you know the great scene where Scarpia wins a woman to his will by sending her lover to the torture chamber, racking her soul with his anguished cries, till she can bear no more. And you have questioned that in the ordeal the woman suffered more.

In the equally terrible tragedy being enacted in Judge Fitzgerald's court, it is the woman who is on the rack—the husband who watches her agony, and perhaps endures a greater agony than she.

There can be no question of Harry Thaw's great love for his wife, his "poor, misguided angel," whose wings were trailed in the dark ooze of the Tenderloin so early.

Love, tenderness, respect for her is breathed in every line of the strange, rambling, incoherent letters he wrote her. And the strength of that love can be the only measure of the torture he endured during her story.

Perhaps, though, he realized that in the hushed silence of the awful moment when Evelyn Thaw's slain innocence rose from its tomb to bear eternal witness against its slayer all individualities were merged, all identities lost. We were no longer men and women in that room. Words fell on women's ears that they had never heard. Vice stalked in naked hideousness before them, yet they were not ashamed. They did not shrink from the men who heard it and saw these horrors, too. They had forgotten them. Before that tragedy of outraged womanhood, conventions were swept away. And each man, each woman in the court-room heard Evelyn Thaw's story as if it were addressed to them alone. And they believed it. Later doubts may have crept into some minds, questions of probability may have assailed them. But for one moment every one thought it true.[70]

The day proved a tremendous ordeal for Evelyn. The next day, Friday, she discussed her return from Europe and the insistence by Stanford White that she never see Thaw again.

"Did you ever see a pistol in Mr. Thaw's possession?"

"Yes," replied Evelyn.

"When for the first time?"

"I don't exactly remember the date. It was in New York, and it was after Christmas Eve, 1903."[71]

Delmas had no further questions, and Evelyn's sensational testimony ended.

The burning question of the day was not Evelyn's integrity as a witness but the need for censorship of her testimony as it was published in the newspapers. To the scandalized protests of President Roosevelt and others, an editorial writer for the *World* gave one of the most thoughtful replies:

The Thaw trial will have done a permanently valuable service if it destroys the veil of secrecy with which public modesty has surrounded certain vices. . . . There are certain matters which every boy or girl is sure to learn about. The alternative is not that of knowledge or ignorance, but whether they will acquire their knowledge from their parents, their school teachers, their physicians and their clergymen, or from the slime of the gutter. . . . The more frankly, baldly and repulsively these facts are taught, the more repellent to vice will be their effect. To paraphrase the Thaw testimony detracts from its educational power. A bald fact cannot be lascivious or suggestive. A paraphrase may be prurient. The stenographer's pencil is not.[72]

NOTES

1. *New York Times*, 25 June 1906.
2. Michael McDonald Mooney, *Evelyn Nesbit and Stanford White* (New York: William Morrow, 1976), p. 219.
3. Charles C. Baldwin, *Stanford White* (New York: Dodd, Mead, 1931), p. 303.
4. Mooney, *Evelyn Nesbit and Stanford White*, p. 223.
5. Evelyn Nesbit, *Prodigal Days* (New York: Julian Messner, 1934), p. 172.
6. Mooney, *Evelyn Nesbit and Stanford White*, p. 221.
7. Ibid., p. 222.
8. *New York Evening World*, 5 February 1907.
9. Baldwin, *Stanford White*, p. 8.
10. Ibid., p. 39.
11. Ibid., p. 115.
12. Ibid., p. 116.
13. Ibid., p. 265.
14. Ibid., p. 175.
15. Ibid., p. 176.
16. Mooney, *Evelyn Nesbit and Stanford White*, p. 183.
17. Ibid., p. 186.
18. Frederick Collins, *Glamorous Sinners* (New York: Ray Long and Richard Smith, 1932), p. 47.
19. Ibid., p. 53.
20. *New York Evening Journal*, 6 August 1906.
21. Mooney, *Evelyn Nesbit and Stanford White*, p. 25.

22. Evelyn Nesbit, *Prodigal Days* (New York: Julian Messner, Inc., 1934), p. 22.

23. *New York Evening World*, 7 February 1907.

24. *New York Journal*, 22 February 1907.

25. Nesbit, *Prodigal Days*, p. 28.

26. Ibid., p. 32.

27. Mooney, *Evelyn Nesbit and Stanford White*, p. 81.

28. Ibid., p. 83.

29. Ibid.

30. Ibid.

31. *New York Evening Journal*, 23 January 1907.

32. Nesbit, *Prodigal Days*, p. 52.

33. Ibid., p. 110.

34. *Pittsburgh Morning Telegraph*, 4 June 1906.

35. Mooney, *Evelyn Nesbit and Stanford White*, p. 225.

36. *New York Evening World*, 5 February 1907.

37. Mooney, *Evelyn Nesbit and Stanford White*, p. 226.

38. *New York Evening World*, 5 February 1907.

39. Langford, *The Murder of Stanford White*, p. 20.

40. Mooney, *Evelyn Nesbit and Stanford White*, p. 226.

41. *New York Evening World*, 26 June 1906.

42. *New York Journal*, 26 June 1906.

43. Mooney, *Evelyn Nesbit and Stanford White*, p. 20.

44. *New York Journal*, 30 June 1906.

45. Mooney, *Evelyn Nesbit and Stanford White*, p. 62.

46. *New York Journal*, 28 June 1906.

47. Ibid., 23 January 1907.

48. *New York Times*, 23 January 1907.

49. Ross, *Ladies of the Press*, p. 65.

50. Ibid., p. 32.

51. Mooney, *Evelyn Nesbit and Stanford White*, p. 62.

52. *New York Evening World*, 23 January 1907.

53. Nesbit, *Prodigal Days*, p. 196.

54. Mooney, *Evelyn Nesbit and Stanford White*, p. 275.

55. *New York Evening World*, 24 January 1907.

56. Ibid.

57. *New York Evening World*, 30 January 1907.

58. *New York Journal*, 26 January 1907.

59. Ibid.

60. *New York American*, 26 January 1907.

61. Langford, *The Murder of Stanford White*, p. 70.

62. *New York Journal*, 6 February 1907.

63. Ibid., 22 January 1907.

64. Ibid., 19 January 1907.
65. *New York Evening World*, 5 February 1907.
66. Ibid., 8 February 1907.
67. *New York Evening World*, 7 February 1907.
68. *New York American*, 8 February 1907.
69. Langford, *The Murder of Stanford White*, p. 119.
70. *New York Evening World*, 8 February 1907.
71. Langford, *The Murder of Stanford White*, p. 126.
72. *New York Evening World*, 11 September 1907.

Chapter 5

The Case: Alienists

Before Evelyn would face cross examination by the district attorney, Delmas tried to demonstrate the effect of her confession to Thaw on his mental state. To do so he called Dr. Britton D. Evans, "A handsome gentleman with a florid face and an agreeable manner."[1] Evans was at the mental hospital at Morris Plains, New Jersey. On his visit to the Tombs, he testified:

Thaw called White this creature, this beast, this vulture, and declared that he sought out only women that were pure in mind as well as body; that he never met a good woman that he did not try to undermine her virtue, and that he, Thaw felt that he had a sacred mission to save women from White.

"I never wanted to shoot White," Evans said Thaw told him, "I never wanted to kill him, I wanted to punish him by legal means. I knew he was devouring the daughters of America, but I wanted to stop him by having him arrested and tried, and disgraced and put in prison."

"I went to see Mr. Comstock about it, and to see Mr. Jerome, and I put Pinkerton detectives upon his track, but they could get no evidence that would warrant me in having him arrested. And Mr. Jerome told me I had better give it up; that there was nothing to it."

"But at last Providence took charge of it. Providence made me the agent for removing him. It wasn't my judgment. I thought it would have been better to do it through a court of law, but I think now that killing him was a better way. If he had lived he would have gotten out of the penitentiary."

Then he spoke of the various girls that had suffered as his wife did at White's hands, and he said that he felt it was his duty to look after them and help them lead moral lives. Never once, according to the physician's testimony, did he manifest the slightest interest in his own welfare, or any apprehension of what might come to him as a result of having committed murder.

He also entertained the delusion that he was being watched and followed by a gang of thugs employed by White, and for that reason always carried a pistol when in New York.[2]

Evans unhesitatingly declared that Thaw had just passed through an explosive and fulminating condition of the mind. He was struck by the "glaring restlessness of Thaw's eyes, by the incoherent flow of his words and by a brainstorm or mental explosion." The term "brainstorm" became a kind of "catch phrase" destined for permanence in the language.[3]

On Thursday the trial was interrupted by the death of Juror Joseph B. Bolton's wife, who for several days had been ill with pneumonia. Dorothy Dix, in true sob sister fashion, wrote a moving account of the event:

Tears are the touch of nature that makes the whole world kin. From our brother's joy we stand aloof—we have no part in it—but in his sorrow we are partners, remembering our own griefs, or in fear of that which may yet befall us.

So it was that yesterday a wave of loving kindness and human tenderness softened for awhile the rigor of the Thaw trial when the news was received that the wife of Juror Bolton was dead. Mr. Jerome made the announcement of the sad event in a wonderfully sympathetic little speech, full of delicacy and fine feeling, and Justice Fitzgerald, in granting an adjournment of court until Monday, removed the ban that has kept the jurors imprisoned, locked up away from home and business for three weeks, so that the bereaved man might be alone with his loss, with no prying eye to take note of his despair.

There had been a piteous little scene that had gone straight home to every heart at the opening of court. It was known that Mrs. Bolton was desperately ill with pneumonia, and there had been some speculation as to whether, on that account, there would be any session or not, but promptly at half-past ten twelve jurors marched solemnly in.

Scarcely, however, had the ponderous wheels of justice begun to slowly turn, when a messenger entered hurriedly and whispered to the judge, whose eyes instinctively turned to-ward the jury box. There sat a little, white-haired, white-faced man, whose face turned still whiter and whiter, until it was ghastly with fear and foreboding, for he knew that the sum-mons expected had come.

He made no outcry, but in that moment he looked old and stricken, and then he stumbled out of the jury box, and somehow, someway, the official forms were gone through, and he started back to that home that had been left to him desolate.

What adds to the pathos of the situation is that Mr. and Mrs. Bolton are said to have been a peculiarly devoted couple. In all the years of married life they have scarcely been parted a day until the beginning of the Thaw trial, when Mr. Bolton was chosen on the jury and locked up with his fellows. Mrs. Bolton has long been a semi invalid, very frail, very delicate, and very dependent on her husband, who guarded and pro-tected her as if she had been a child. It was her desire to see him that indirectly caused her death, as she braved the storm of last week to go down to the Broadway Central Hotel to visit him and the exposure of the trip resulted in the attack of pneumonia that proved fatal to her.

We share the grief and despair of this poor husband and wife, who in the supreme hour were parted, while the one went down into the Valley of the Shadow alone, the other

gnawed his heart out in impotent despair because he might
not be with her and comfort her for that dread journey.[4]

Juror Bolton had returned to the courtroom on Monday in time for
Jerome's interrogation to begin. Jerome's objective was to obtain a
conviction. In order to do so he had to prove either that Evelyn had
not told Thaw the story she claimed she had after his proposal of
marriage, or else that her story had not temporarily affected Thaw's
mind. Since he could not produce such proof, he had to attempt to
impugn Evelyn's character and her integrity as a witness. Still wearing
her navy blue suit with the stiff-collared shirt waist, she seated herself
in the witness stand and the cross examination began:

Q. Up until the time you went into the Floradora Company in 1901, had you
    ever posed in the nude?
A. Never.
Q. Did you not have a plaster cast of yourself in the nude made in the spring
    of 1901?
A. I did not.
Q. Did you know of a Mr. Wells, a sculptor?
A. No, I never heard of him.

During this questioning Jerome had referred to a document he
had in his hand, clearly a psychological ploy to disarm Evelyn. His
questioning took an abrupt change:

Q. Up until the time when he [Thaw] offered his hand to you in marriage, had
    you believed there was nothing wrong in the relations between men and
    women?
A. I knew it was wrong. Oh yes, I knew that—I knew from what I heard the
    girls say in the theatre.
Q. Would you say that up until 1903 you merely esteemed them as vulgar and
    indelicate?
A. I would say that I thought them wrong.

During Jerome's inquisition, as it came to be called, Nixola Greeley-Smith was reminded of a large cat just getting ready to devour a

fluttering helpless little bird. "The rare quality of her beauty seemed to shrivel like cherry blossoms when a vagrant March wind strays into May. Today the stamp of terror is upon it still."[5]

Q. Had you ever had any religious instruction?
A. No—none at all.
Q. And you were then more than eighteen years old?
A. Yes, over eighteen.
Q. Did you believe in the existence of a Divine Being?
A. I could not say whether I did or not.
Q. Did you begin then to appreciate the terrible wrong you say Stanford White did to you?

Evelyn sensing a trap was ready with an answer.

A. I saw it all better after Mr. Thaw proposed to me and we talked it all over. I know better now how wrong I was treated, but all along I realized something about it.
Q. When you told Mr. Thaw the reason why you would not marry him that time in Paris it was because you loved him, was it not?

Winfred Black sloppily describes her answer:

Evelyn Thaw raised her tilted, delicate little face as I have seen a frail meadow flower raise its perfumed head when someone passes quickly by. She looked over at her husband and smiled a little wistful smile such as you see on the face of the little girl when she wants to propitiate her big brother and get him not to tell Momma what she has been doing. "It was because I loved him" said the witness, and Harry Thaw's broad, white face overspread with a sudden flush and his big dull eyes grew all at once absolutely brilliant.[6]

Jerome dropped the point, but it had been a narrow escape for Evelyn. In her earlier testimony she had stated that she had accepted White's assurance that nearly all women were unchaste. The question Jerome had wanted to ask was why she had refused Thaw's proposal if at the time she had believed herself no less worthy than most other women. Her belated explanation that her affairs with White had become public knowledge was quick thinking.[7]

Jerome switched his line of questioning to the night of Evelyn's alleged seduction by White.

Q. How long were you unconscious in the Twenty-fourth Street studio when you were with Mr. White?

A. I don't know.

Q. Was it after midnight?

A. Yes.

Q. You said that you did not recall how you got your clothes on. White went away and left you, and you sat up all night. Now when did you finally get home?

A. That I cannot remember.

After a few more questions designed to suggest that the evening's experience was less traumatic than would be expected, Jerome turned to her sense of propriety. Winifred Black claims that he did his best—his satirical, biting, disagreeable best—to break down the witness.[8]

Q. Did you love Stanford White?

A. No.

Q. You hated him?

A. Yes.

Q. Yet, you didn't feel outraged at the time you met Thaw—not until he told you how wrong it was?

A. No.

Q. You didn't feel outraged when a man you describe as a big, yellow brute drugged you and wronged you?

A. Yes, I did.

Q. Did you drink to excess with White?

A. Yes.

Q. Were you inebriated? [Referring to her seduction by White].

A. Yes.

Q. Did you tell your mother?

A. No.

Q. Did you ever tell any human being?

A. No.

Q. You always resisted and never submitted willingly?

A. I always resisted. I did not like it.

Q. You are sure you were always under the influence of liquor?

A. Yes.

By now Evelyn was in tears, and her answers came faintly. Undeterred, Jerome pressed on in order to continue in his attempt to defame her character. "The Spaniards of the Middle Ages, geniuses of inventive cruelty, could not have devised tortures more ingenious than the prosecution plied the girl with today," complained Ada Patterson in the *New York American*.[9]

Q. When you first met Stanford White did you know he was a married man?

A. No.

Q. Were there any improprieties at this first meeting at the tower?

A. Mr. White kissed me.

Q. That didn't offend your maidenly modesty at the time?

A. I don't remember. I know now that it was not right. He seemed very kind and fatherly. He always treated me just like a father except in the way he took advantage of me. Outside of this awful part of his life he was very nice, very kind, and except in one way he was very good to me. . . . Outside of that one terrible thing Stanford White was a very grand man. . . . I told this to Mr. Thaw—about Mr. White's kind and fatherly manner—and he said that it only made him all the more dangerous. Harry said that him being so kind and considerate only made him the more dangerous to the community.

Q. Did you, after being wronged, continue to go out to dinner and to dinner parties with Stanford White?

A. Often. Sometimes every day, sometimes two or three times a week.

Q. When was it that you refused positively to continue the practice of going to his room or seeing him alone?

A. It was January 1903, I think.

Q. Did he coax you often?

A. Yes, very often. He would scold me and grow very unpleasant if I tried to refuse.

Q. Did he continue to give you money during the period that these improper relations were maintained?

A. Yes, he gave me money a number of times during 1901, during 1902, and once or twice, I think, early in 1903—over a year in all, I think.

Jerome's questioning continued, switching from point to point. He got her to admit that while being supported by White, she once spent three days in Philadelphia, where—with two other girls—she visited the home of an unnamed man. He continued to probe her premarital promiscuity.

Jerome, at this point, called for Dr. Carlton Flint, rumored to be the physician to whom John Barrymore had taken Evelyn for professional services of a questionable nature.

Q. Did you ever see this gentleman before?

A. No.

Q. Are you sure?

A. I am quite sure I never saw him before.

Q. Did you go to that gentleman for medical treatment in this city?

A. No sir.

Q. Did you not go with Jack Barrymore to this Dr. Carlton Flint's office in his home in New York City?

A. No sir.

Q. Was the operation performed on you at the Pompton school a criminal operation?

Delmas objected to the question, pointing out that Evelyn had been under an anesthetic and could have known only what was told to her about the operation—that it was an appendectomy.

Before ending his cross examination, the district attorney seemed to abandon his attempt to discredit Evelyn. He had a complete change of strategy. He discussed Thaw's alleged insanity and encouraged Evelyn to testify to several instances of irrational conduct before the murder. His change of strategy appeared to most observers to be an admission of defeat.

On the last day of Evelyn's cross examination District Attorney Jerome produced her diary, written when she was a sixteen-year-old student at the De Mille School in 1902. He read aloud several passages written in a "seemingly sophisticated, superficially clever patter that one girl in musical comedy picks up from another. . . . Considering the terrible experiences related by young Mrs. Thaw as having occurred before the writing of this diary, its tone is singularly light-hearted and wholesome."[10] Nixola Greeley-Smith rationalized that the diary was a "quaint and rather piteous human document, an odd mixture of childish naivete and Tenderloin slang, of old world cynicism and girlish sentiment, with through it all running a dim, wondering, dawning sense of something higher and better in life than she had known. Most of the entries in the journal are perfunctory little references to the day's doings."[11] The spectacle proved unendurable for Nixola Greeley-Smith, who commented:

Several hundred years ago when persons under suspicion of the law refused to confess their guilt they were tortured by the authorities until they admitted it.

Justice no longer tortures the body. The rack and thumb-screw are things of the past. Yet it is difficult to imagine greater suffering than that inflicted in the name of the law in Justice Fitzgerald's court yesterday upon Evelyn Nesbit Thaw.

Here was the vivisection of a woman's soul, the tearing from it of its profoundest secrets, a rending, wrenching, merciless digging into its depths that by comparison made the rack seem less hideous and awful.

No one believes that District Attorney Jerome likes his task, and in describing the agony which this young woman is made to suffer under cross-examination I am offering no criticism of the methods which, I suppose, he considers it his duty to the people of New York to employ.

I simply feel that compared with the ordeal to which the frail young woman was subjected, a prize-fight might be an elevating spectacle, and a day at the Chicago stockyards a pastoral delight.

Before an audience of many hundred men young Mrs. Thaw was compelled to reveal in all its hideousness every detail of her association with Stanford White after his crime against her. Not once, but many times. Over and over and over again came the same revolting questions, the same trembling, piteous answers.

It seemed as if, in his effort to overcome the young woman's story, Mr. Jerome had dragnetted the sewers of the world for crude words, raw phrases that cut the tortured soul as the knot draws blood from the tortured body, to hurl at the quivering woman on the witness stand.[12]

Following the cross examination of Evelyn it was now Delmas's turn. He called Mrs. William Thaw to the stand. Wrote the columnist Ada Patterson:

The elder Mrs. Thaw will leave the chair where she has sat patiently, watchful, in silence eloquent of pain and tears, to be hidden in an adjoining room, where again she will wait, agonizingly and prayerfully, for her chance to help her boy in his peril. It has been determined that she will go upon the stand. She will be the chief witness for the defense. To save her son from the electric chair she will crucify her soul upon the cross of memory.

For the mother will be made to tell, bit by bit, fitting the broken pieces of the story together in a mosaic of miserable recollections, how her son from his infancy was cursed by a warped mind. She will repeat, in parallel, Ibsen's "Ghosts."[13]

Dressed in her "widow's weeds—black furs around her shoulders, an unadorned black dress, black kid gloves—and her low-pitched dowager's voice," Mrs. Thaw faced her questioner.[14] Delmas began:

Q. At what time in the fall of 1903 did your son, Harry K. Thaw, come to your house?
A. Some time in November.
Q. Did you notice any change in his manner?

A. Yes. His manner was utterly different from what it had been before he went away. He had a staring look and he seemed to have lost interest in everything. . . . He was very fond of music, and soon after he came home he went into the drawing room. He began playing in a very violent manner. One night, after all had retired, I heard smothered groans, I went to the door and heard that he was sobbing. He told me he could not sleep. And I asked him what was the matter. He said that there was something on his mind that kept sleep away. You can tell your mother, can't you? No, it is a story I can tell no one.

Q. You have stated, Madam that you observed that your son was often awake until two o'clock. Did he ever tell you what it was that kept him awake?

A. He did not tell me all, only a little. He said that he was troubled by the thought of a wicked thing the wickedest man in New York had done. He said that this man had ruined his life. He said that he would never get over it, that he couldn't keep it out of his mind, and that it would not let him sleep.

Q. Did you get any further information at that time?

A. No, but later he told me more. On Thanksgiving Day of that year I learned very much more. I had not then learned the girl's name; I knew that there must be a girl in it, nor did I want to know. But at Thanksgiving time I heard more from him. I went to him one night and asked him what it was that had happened. Why should your life be ruined? Then he said to me that a certain man had ruined the girl whom he loved and that his life was spoiled. This, I recall, was just before Thanksgiving.

Q. You said, Mrs. Thaw, that he said it was something a wicked man had done in New York that distressed him?

A. Yes. He said a wicked man, probably the worst man in New York, was to blame. He said this man had wronged a young girl. He did not tell me the young girl's name at that time. I did not ask him who the young girl was. I did not want to know, as I have just told you. I did not care to know, not then. He told me that he thought this young girl had the most beautiful mind of any young girl he had ever known. He said he would make it his business to see that this girl was not dragged down.

Q. Did your son refer again to the condition of this young girl and her misfortune?

A. He did so frequently. It would be impossible for me to name the different occasions.

Q. When did you learn who this young girl was?

A. In the spring of 1904, I think.

Q. What was it he told you about this young girl?

A. He told me about how she had posed for various artists, finally going to New York, where she went on the stage. There she had met the wicked man he spoke. . . . When he came back [from Europe]. . . . There was a horrible scandal about the ruin of this girl. It was terrible. I remember expressing my disapproval of his coming back on the same steamer with the girl, and I also spoke of certain rumors that had been sent from the other side. He said there was nothing wrong in his actions and that these rumors were untrue.

Q. Did he express his desire to marry her as early as the fall of 1903?

A. Yes, I think he did. I did not approve until March, 1905, about two months before the wedding. Seeing how he felt, I told him that it was probably the least of two evils, and that he had better marry her. I told him the question was one for him to decide. Then he asked me if I would go to New York and see her. I said I would. I told him he did not need my approbation, that the matter was one for him to decide.

Q. So you finally gave your consent to have the marriage take place in your home?

A. Yes.

Delmas had no further questions. Jerome cross-examined the witness only perfunctorily, and she was excused.

"Isn't there anything else?" she asked, turning to Delmas.

"No, madam, that is all."

"I want to ask for an opportunity to say something in regard to heredity," Mrs. Thaw persisted.

"No, no, madam. We desire that nothing further be asked of you at this time."

"But I wanted to tell these gentlemen—I wanted to correct some false impressions."

Delmas strongly urged Mrs. Thaw to please refrain. "There is nothing more that you should say in this court to this jury."

Ada Patterson had reported that:

Secretly, diligently, day after day, hour after hour, her agents [Mrs. William Thaw's], directed by private letters and cipher code dispatches from her, have sought in Pittsburgh corroborative proof of the story she wanted to tell. They had sought and found friends who remember Harry Thaw in his boyhood, who

could recall him even as an infant, and every one has some story
to tell of the strange obsessions and the curious hallucinations of
William Thaw's strange son, Harry. This mass of evidence and
corroborative testimony was not to be entered.[15]

Mrs. Thaw's testimony had a great effect on Nixola Greeley-Smith:

The second great occasion of the trial had come, and Thaw's
mother met it, determination written large on her placid
forehead, the light of battle in her mild blue eyes. . . . Mrs.
Thaw carries on her silver hair the crown of noble motherhood—of womanhood sheltered and respected and esteemed
by all men, and she is not unaware of it. . . . The jurors listened
to the story told by Mrs. Thaw with respectful inten-
tions . . . [and] believed every word, as everyone must have
believed who heard it.[16]

"When Mr. Delmas's bow of dismissal notified her that her
ordeal was over she smiled, drew her coat and her fur collar about
her and walked to the door of the witness room."[17]

Jerome's attempt to prove Thaw sane and guilty of premeditated
murder was proving unsuccessful, and the case of the prosecution
was looking hopeless until Jerome won the argument and Abraham
Hummel, whose testimony Delmas had successfully blocked earlier, was allowed to testify for the prosecution.

Q. Did you after your conversation with Evelyn Nesbit dictate something to a
    stenographer?

A. Yes, I did.

Q. Did she state that Thaw wanted to injure White and put him in the
    penitentiary? Did she tell you Thaw had prepared documents accusing
    White of having drugged and ruined her? Did she tell you Thaw had beaten
    her because she had refused to sign this document, and she said White was
    not guilty?

A. In effect, yes, she did.

Q. Thereafter in her presence and hearing did you dictate something to a
    stenographer? Can you recall what it was that you dictated?

A. I can so recall. . . .
Q. I now hand you exhibit 77 [the dictated affidavit] and ask you if you ever saw this before.
A. Yes, sir.
Q. Where?
A. In my office in October of 1903.
Q. What became of it finally?
A. I gave it to Evelyn Nesbit in my office.
Q. Did you ever see it again?
A. I never did.

The document, containing the facts which Evelyn had told Hummel—which he had incorporated into an affidavit in 1903—was now introduced as evidence. It read as follows:

SUPREME COURT, COUNTY OF NEW YORK
EVELYN NESBIT, PLAINTIFF
AGAINST
HARRY KENDALL THAW, DEFENDANT
City and County of New York, ss.:

Evelyn Nesbit, being duly sworn, says: I reside at the Savoy Hotel, Fifth Avenue and Fifty-ninth Street, in the city of New York. I am eighteen years of age, having been born on Christmas Day, in the year 1884.

For several months prior to June, 1903, I had been at Dr. Bull's Hospital, at No. 33 West Thirty-third Street, in this city, where I had had an operation performed on me for appendicitis, and during the month of June went to Europe with my mother, at the request of Harry Kendall Thaw, the defendant above named. My mother and I had apartments on the Avenue Mantignon, in Paris, France, and from there traveled to Boulogne, during which we were accompanied by Mr. Thaw. Mr. Thaw left at once for London, England, while my mother and I remained at the Imperial Hotel about three weeks.

While the said Thaw was in London he wrote me a number of letters. He then returned to Boulogne and took my mother and myself back to Paris, where we stayed at the Langham Hotel. We lived there about two weeks, after which the said Thaw, my mother and I returned to London, where we located at the Claridge Hotel—that is, my mother and I lived at that place, while Mr. Thaw stayed at the Carlton Hotel, in the city of London.

My mother remained at Claridge's Hotel for some little time and then moved to the Russell Square Hotel, in Russell Square, London. I went with Mr. Thaw to Amsterdam, Holland, by way of Folkestone.

I was ill during this entire period. Mr. Thaw and I then traveled throughout Holland, stopping at various places to catch connecting trains, and then we went to Munich, Germany. We then traveled through the Bavarian Highlands, finally going to the Austrian Tyrol. During all this time the said Thaw and myself were known as husband and wife, and were represented by the said Thaw and known under the name of Mr. and Mrs. Dellis.

After traveling together about five or six weeks, the said Thaw rented a castle in the Austrian Tyrol, known as the Schloss Katzenstein, which is situated about half way up a very isolated mountain. This castle must have been built centuries ago, as the rooms and windows are all old-fashioned. When we reached there, there were a number of servants in the castle, but the only servants I saw were a butler, the cook and the maid. We occupied one entire end of the castle, consisting of two bedrooms, a parlor and a drawing room, which were used by us. The balance of the house was rented by the said Thaw, but was not occupied by us. I was assigned a bedroom for my personal use.

The first night we reached the "schloss" I was very tired and went to bed right after dinner. In the morning I was awakened by Mr. Thaw pounding on the door and asking me to come to breakfast, saying the coffee was getting cold. I immediately jumped out of bed and hastily put on a bathrobe and slippers. I walked out of my room and sat down to breakfast with the said Thaw.

After breakfast the said Thaw said he wished to tell me something, and asked me to step into my bedroom. I entered the room, when the said Thaw, without any provocation, grasped me by the throat and tore the bathrobe from my body, leaving me entirely nude except for my slippers. I saw by his face that the said Thaw was in a terrific, excited condition, and I was terrorized. His eyes were glaring, and he had in his right hand a cowhide whip. He seized hold of me and threw me on the bed. I was powerless and attempted to scream, but the said Thaw placed his fingers in my mouth and tried to choke me. He then, without any provocation and without the slightest reason, began to inflict on me several severe and violent blows with the cowhide whip. So brutally did he assault me that my skin was cut and bruised. I besought him to desist, but he refused. I was so exhausted that I shouted and cried. He stopped every minute or so to rest, and then renewed his attack upon me, which he continued for about seven minutes.

He acted like a demented man. I was absolutely in fear of my life; the servants could not hear my outcries. . . . The said Thaw threatened to kill me, and by reason of his brutal attack, as I have described, I was unable to move. . . . The following morning Thaw again came into my bedroom and administered a castigation similar to the day before. . . .

It was nearly three weeks before I was sufficiently recovered to be able to get out of my bed and walk. When I did so, the said Thaw took me to a place called the Ortier Mountain, where Italy, Switzerland and Germany conjoin. Then we went into Switzerland. In Switzerland we remained at the Hotel Schweitzerhof that night, at Santa Maria. The next morning I made some remark, and the said Thaw took a rattan whip, and while I was in my nightgown, beat me over the leg below the knee so violently that I screamed for help. When I began to scream, the said Thaw again stuffed his fingers in my mouth. During all the time I traveled with the said Thaw, he would make the slightest pretext an excuse for a terrific assault on me. . . .

One day my maid was in my room taking things out of the drawers and packing them away. I found a little silver box, oblong in shape, and about two and a half inches long, containing a hypodermic syringe and some other small utensils. I went to the said Thaw and asked him what it was and what it meant, and he then stated to me that he had been ill, and tried to make some excuse, saying he had been compelled to use cocaine.

I realized then, for the first time, that the said Thaw was addicted to the cocaine habit. I also frequently saw the said Thaw administer cocaine to himself internally by means of small pills. On one occasion he attempted to force me to take one of these pills, but I refused to do so. . . . During this entire period, while I was in this condition of non-resistance Thaw entered my bed and without my consent repeatedly wronged me. I reproved the said Thaw for his conduct, but he compelled me to submit thereto, threatening to beat and kill me if I did not do so. . . .

I have not seen my mother since I left her in London, and am informed within the past two weeks that she returned to the city of New York from London on the steamship Compania. . . .

I have been repeatedly told by the said Thaw that he is very inimical to a married man, whom, he said, he wanted me to injure, and that he, Thaw, would get him into the penitentiary; and the said Thaw has begged me time and again to swear to written documents which he had prepared, involving this married man and charging him with drugging me and having betrayed me when I was fifteen years of age. This was not so; and so I told him, but because I refused to sign these papers, the said Thaw not alone threatened me with bodily injury, but inflicted on me the great bodily injury I have herein described.

(Signed) Evelyn Nesbit

Howe & Hummell, attorneys for the plaintiff.[18]

Dorothy Dix sadly proclaimed that the affidavit:

turns the coldest, cruelest light yet shed upon Evelyn and
Harry Thaw. At its best it shows Evelyn Nesbit lying to Thaw
in Paris or lying to White in New York while she lived
luxuriously on the money of both and it shows Thaw as either
completely her dupe or else planning one of the most das-
tardly and cowardly acts on record, that of getting even with
the enemy by dragging a young girl through the mire.

Undoubtedly all of these things have weakened sympathy
with Thaw and when the state closed its case the unwritten
law seemed but the ghost of a dead hand fighting against the
fist of the written law that had smitten it fist and thigh.[19]

By now—for what it was worth—Jerome had succeeded in casting
considerable doubt on the truth of the story Evelyn said she had
told Thaw in Paris.

Jerome once again reversed his strategy. To Judge Fitzgerald's
surprise Jerome in a fervent speech stated:

"There is not a man who has sat in this room during these
eight weeks and looked at that man," Jerome cried turning
and pointing a shaking finger at Thaw, "who does not know
that he is crazy and that we have been engaged in a disgraceful
procedure in trying him for his life. I have believed from the
first that the prisoner was insane, and the record will bear me
out that I have tried time and again to have the state of his
mind determined before we went any further, but the counsel
has blocked my every move, and kept back the evidence that
I had, and I have been forced to go on with proof in my
possession that would stop this miserable farce, and that I
could not get before the court. It is true I feel bitterly on this
subject.

I feel so bitterly that I have served notice on the counsel
for the defense that after this trial was over if I found out that
they had information in their possession that I believed they

had, I might call the attention of the Appellate Division of the Supreme Court to their conduct.

We have no right to be trying this man, and I appeal to the conscience of the court to stop this trial until we can investigate into the sanity of the prisoner.[20]

Dorothy Dix in her amazement at the turn of events wrote:

Never was there such a turning of tables and shifting of positions as there has been in this case, and the end of the fifth week of the trial finds that the prosecution and defense have practically swapped places as regards the mental condition of the accused man. It is the State now that is trying to prove that Harry Thaw is insane and has been mentally unbalanced for years, while the Thaw lawyers are battling with might and main to show that he is rational.[21]

A lunacy commission was appointed, composed of the following three members: Peter B. Olney, a well-known lawyer and former district attorney of New York; Dr. Leonard Putzel, an eminent specialist in mental disease; and, as chairman, David McClure, another prominent lawyer, who represented the Catholic diocese of Manhattan in legal matters.[22]

Thaw issued a statement to the press: "I am perfectly sane, and everybody who knows me know that I am sane. In fact, on second consideration of the matters, I am rather glad, on the whole, that the case has taken this turn, because I am satisfied the commission in lunacy is going to declare that I am sane at present, and after that you can guess for yourself what will happen."[23]

The commission deliberated for seven days.[24] The first order of business was a two-hour examination of Thaw. His responses were so coherent and rational that before the end of the preliminary examination Jerome announced that he had lost interest in the attempt to prove Thaw insane and that he would bring forward no witnesses of his own.[25]

By unanimous vote the commission pronounced Thaw sane. On Monday, April 8, with court back in session, Delmas began his memorable summation, which included a discussion of the nature of Thaw's mental condition:

> If Thaw is insane, it is with a species of insanity that is known from the Canadian border to the Gulf. If you expert gentlemen ask me to give it a name, I suggest that you label it *Dementia Americana.* It is that species of insanity that persuades an American that whoever violates the sanctity of his home or the purity of his wife or daughter has forfeited the protection of the laws of this state or any other state.[26]

The following day Jerome presented his summation, and to most his shrewd analysis of Evelyn's character was more convincing than the melodramatic story she had told. But he still did not face the issue at hand—whether Evelyn had told Thaw her story in 1903 and whether it had upset his mental equilibrium.[27]

On the afternoon of April 10 Judge Fitzgerald delivered his charge to the jury. He pointed out that a person did not escape criminal liability on the ground of insanity unless his defective reasoning was such that he did not understand that his action was wrong; that the law presumed sanity and the burden of proof of insanity was on the defense; that the jury must decide whether Thaw knew the act of firing a revolver at an enemy would cause death and was forbidden by law; and that the story told by the defendant's wife about her relationship with Stanford White had not been presented with regard to its truth or falsity but in order that the jury might determine its effect on the defendant's mental condition.[28]

Thirty hours after deliberations began, the jury returned to the courtroom. Judge Fitzgerald asked: "Gentleman, have you reached a verdict?" Foreman Deming B. Smith replied, "We have not." On the final ballot it was learned five had voted him not guilty by reason of insanity and seven had voted him guilty of first-degree murder.[29]

Among the final news items was a statement from Evelyn's mother, quoted in the *Pittsburgh Leader*, denying any previous knowledge of Evelyn's seduction by White. "Had she told me what she told the Thaw jury it would not have been necessary for Harry Thaw to kill Stanford White. I would have done it myself."[30]

Harry Thaw was returned across the Bridge of Sighs to the Tombs where he was to remain until the start of his second trial which officially opened on Monday, January 6, 1908. In his opening statement, Martin W. Littleton, in charge of the defense, stated, "the defendant must plead that he was insane at the time he committed the crime. He need not claim that he was sane or insane before he committed the crime, that he was insane the moment he committed the crime and then, a moment after, sane again. No, he must make the simple claim that at the time he killed Stanford White he was insane."[31]

District Attorney Jerome opened for the prosecution. "Gentlemen of the jury," he said, "we contend that the defendant was sane when he committed the crime. We further contend that it was a premeditated, cowardly murder, and this we shall endeavor to prove."[32]

Jerome's case for first-degree murder was well presented despite his choice not to challenge the testimony of witnesses for the defense who detailed examples of Harry Thaw's history of irrationality.[33] Included were relatives attesting to the incompetence of other relatives, former teachers attesting to his irrational behavior as a student, his mother, who had been seriously ill and remained so feeble that she had to be helped to the stand by a nurse armed with smelling salts. Mrs. William Thaw produced examples of Harry's mental unbalance which she claimed began at three months of age when he displayed signs of nervousness accompanied by screams and twitching limbs. Mrs. Harry Thaw followed her mother-in-law on the witness stand and, in an attempt to prove her husband insane, for the first time in any testimony, revealed Harry's attempted suicide in 1904 while they were visiting Paris.[34]

Several alienists were again asked to testify. Following their testimony, Jerome rose to sum up the case for the people of New

York. Instead of trying to exonerate White or discredit Evelyn, he directed his efforts to an attack on Thaw. Though he had given up hope of convicting Thaw of first-degree murder, he went through necessary arguments against the plea of insanity.

In his summary Littleton spoke of the "hereditary insanity which, working its way to the blood and brain of this defendant, made him nervous, made him mentally unstable, and made him liable to a breakdown under great strain."[35]

On the morning of January 31, 1908, the case went to the jury. Following twenty-four hours of deliberation the jury returned to the courtroom. "Gentlemen," asked Justice Dowling, "have you agreed upon a verdict?"

The foreman said they had, and the clerk of the court called for their verdict, which the foreman then read. "We, the jury, find the defendant not guilty as charged in the indictment on the ground of the defendant's insanity."[36]

Justice Dowling thanked the jury and turned his attention to Thaw. He read a statement prepared in anticipation of this outcome:

The jury having found a verdict that this defendant is not guilty of the murder of Stanford White on the ground of insanity, it now devolves upon the Court to take certain action. The testimony, as brought out by the defense, proves conclusively that this defendant has suffered and still suffers from the form of insanity known as manic-depressive. It appears further that there is danger of further outbreaks on the part of this defendant, just as in the past there have been outbreaks. . . . The Court, therefore, orders that the defendant, being in custody and being a person dangerous to the public safety, the said Harry K. Thaw shall be kept in custody and shall be sent to the Asylum for the Criminal Insane at Matteawan forth with. The Sheriff of New York County is charged with the duty of immediately executing this order.[37]

On February 1, 1908, Harry Thaw hired a private railroad car attached to the train which delivered him to Matteawan.[38]

NOTES

1. *New York Evening World*, 13 February 1907.

2. *New York Journal*, 12 February 1907.

3. Gerald Langford, *The Murder of Stanford White* (Indianapolis: Bobbs-Merrill, 1962), p. 132.

4. *New York Evening World*, 16 February 1907.

5. Ibid., 20 February 1907.

6. *New York Journal*, 20 February 1907.

7. Langford, *The Murder of Stanford White*, p. 147.

8. *New York Journal*, 7 February 1907.

9. *New York American*, 22 February 1907.

10. *New York Evening World*, 27 February 1907.

11. Ibid.

12. Ibid.

13. *New York American*, 1 February 1907.

14. Langford, *The Murder of Stanford White*, p. 174.

15. *New York American*, 1 February 1907.

16. Langford, *The Murder of Stanford White*, p. 180.

17. *New York Journal*, 7 March 1907.

18. *New York Evening Journal*, 19 March 1907.

19. Ibid., 21 March 1907.

20. Ibid., 21 March 1907.

21. Ibid., 22 March 1907.

22. Langford, *The Murder of Stanford White*, p. 199.

23. Michael McDonald Mooney, *Evelyn Nesbit and Stanford White* (New York: William Morrow, 1976), p. 261.

24. Ibid.

25. Langford, *The Murder of Stanford White*, p. 200.

26. *New York Times*, 9 April 1907.

27. *Toledo Blade*, 10 April 1907.

28. Langford, *The Murder of Stanford White*, p. 205.

29. *New York Telegraph*, 12 April 1907.

30. *Pittsburgh Leader*, 10 April 1907.

31. *New York Evening World*, 8 January 1908.

32. Langford, *The Murder of Stanford White*, p. 216.

33. Mooney, *Evelyn Nesbit and Stanford White*, p. 267.

34. Ibid., p. 268.

35. Langford, *The Murder of Stanford White*, p. 231.

36. Mooney, *Evelyn Nesbit and Stanford White*, p. 270.

37. Langford, *The Murder of Stanford White*, p. 234.

38. *New York Evening World*, 1 February 1908.

What factors allowed this new and immensely popular form of journalism to flourish? Why was it so successful in 1907 while it probably would have failed completely a decade earlier?

The turn of the twentieth century, known also as the *fin de siècle* and the Progressive years, marked a time of stock-taking and analysis in the United States. Though struggling with new concepts and a new ideology, the country seemed ready for a fresh start. Gone was the Victorian Era with its strict morality, its simplistic approach to women and the class system, its rigid, almost obsessive orderliness in every facet of life. As though by magic the four numbers one, nine, zero, zero (1900) brought tremendous upheaval in American life-style and thought. Some changes were thrust upon the country by the sheer necessity of technological progress; others were the result of changes in basic attitudes and priorities. The dissemination of information regarding all these new ideas, whether technological or ideological, depended on an expanded, revised, more informative, and more egalitarian press.

A formerly agrarian society had became an urban one. Industrialization required this great shift of people to the cities. Simultaneously, droves of the downtrodden from all over Europe were immigrating to the United States competing for the same living space and jobs. Never before had this country needed to deal with problems such as overpopulation and urban ghettos, assimilation of immigrants, and the rising rate of urban crime. Employers and entrepreneurs took advantage of these adverse circumstances to exploit urban dwellers—working hours and conditions were deplorable, and salaries were pathetically low. Frustration, disappointment, and unhappiness were the inevitable results. Eking out a marginal existence was perhaps all one of these urban dwellers could reasonably expect from life. There were no pleasures, no diversions—except for the newspaper. The newspaper became not only an organ for the dissemination of hard economic and social facts; it also brought hope and allowed an outlet for fantasies. Indeed the newspaper contained news of continued oppression at the workplace, but it also discussed possibilities of unionization and other forms of collective action. There was hope for a better life. Those new mechanical household machines, those processed canned foods, those beautiful ready-made clothes seen in newspaper advertisements provided a paradoxical combination of increased frustration yet an optimism that these products could be someday within their grasp. Stories of the rich and their exciting lives brought not contempt but an almost perverse pleasure in seeing their unattainable "Cinderella at the ball" fantasies being played out.

What fertile ground, therefore, was laid for this new kind of journalism which had its origin telling, in a heartrending and emotional fashion, the trials and tribulations of a young woman who, in order to avoid a life of poverty and oblivion, became involved even sexually with a member of the upper class, married another wealthy person, and then became an innocent bystander to the murder of one of them. Did readers really want to know the precise legal procedures or statutes or precedents regarding the case? No, they wanted to know what this beautiful young thing, who could easily have been one of their sisters or daughters, was wearing, how a tear glistened on her pure white cheek, how she seemed at least thrice weekly on the brink of collapse. Did those poor downtrodden, overworked, underpaid factory workers and immigrants like it? They loved it! They flocked to the newsstands as soon as the bell signaled the end of the workday to ascertain how their Evelyn was faring—to laugh, to scorn and, yes, to *sob*.

Was sob sister journalism appealing only to the lower classes who found an emotional outlet in this reportage? Indeed not. Readers on all social levels, especially women, were not only amused but emotionally and intellectually involved in sob sister reporting. The Victorian ideals of virtue and womanhood had faded. The early twentieth century precursor of what in the 1960s came to be known as "women's liberation" had taken hold. Middle-class women sought education and were seeking status as professionals. They became deeply involved in the Progressive reform movement addressing such new issues as women's suffrage, pornography, and equal rights. Radical groups were organized to challenge the relegation of economic and social institutions to the all-male domain. Relationships between husbands and wives were reassessed. Premarital sexual purity was no longer sacred although promiscuity was not exactly *de rigueur*. Thus, it is clear why sob sister journalism might appeal to this vast group of women. While scorning it as impure journalism and ridiculing of women on the one hand, the reformers saw this trial and the way it was covered as a microcosm of all the social issues they were trying to bring to the attention of the American public. This was, in a sense, free advertising. While readers sobbed at the daily coverage, perhaps, at least subliminally, they were attaining an awareness of the plight of women in society. It is not inconceivable that some of these middle-class reformers also became emotionally involved themselves and were not as intellectually distant as they may have pretended.

Sob sister journalism held appeal for upper-class women as well. There was the obvious titillation and morbid curiosity about the personal lives of some of "their own." Many of these people were habitués of the new cabarets and roof-garden restaurants like the one where the murder occurred. How could they not be curious about Stanford White's escapades and the lurid details of his murder? How could they not speculate about how this would affect the social standing of the widow White and the Thaws themselves—Harry's mother and his sisters, the Countess of Yarmouth and Mrs. George Lauder Carnegie? Every bit of posturing, every grimace or smile, every detail of clothing, jewelry, and makeup acquired great significance and were discussed by these women, their hairdressers and couturieres. Who looked peaked, who was composed, who trembled were topics of conversation at tea time in drawing rooms and country clubs (even men's clubs) throughout the country. Of course, for the record, sob sister journalism was seen by high society as degrading and plebeian, but there is little doubt that this new form of writing was received with great interest, if not with sheer delight.

It is unfair to speculate that all upper-class interest in sob sister journalism was voyeuristic and prurient. Upper-class women had also found their traditional roles lost with the waning of Victorian thinking and the advent of industrialization. Being the "lady of the manor" was no longer the great virtue it had been. Furthermore, mechanization had provided processed foods and ready-to-wear clothes. These factors allowed the upper-class woman a good deal more time, and some involved themselves in charitable projects that attempted to afford solutions to the problems plaguing the overworked, the unhealthy, the underfed, and the unassimilated. Settlement houses were founded and other charities were established. To these women sob sister journalism would become an avenue to increase public awareness of social ills.

Sob sister journalism could not have started without profound changes in the press itself. The press, too, responded to and perhaps even caused some of the great changes occurring in America at the fin de siècle. Industrialization and urbanization, immigration, the Progressive political scene, the changing morality, the shifting role of women were all significant trends that exerted a deep influence on the American press.

Between 1892 and 1914 the number of daily newspapers increased from 1,650 to 2,250 with a total increase of 100 percent in circulation as opposed to a 50 percent increase in population.[2] Newspapers had become big business. "The magnitude of financial operations of the newspaper is turning journalism upside down," wrote Lincoln Steffens.[3]

After 1900 the increasing size and complexity of the newspaper business plus the advent of large-scale financing were powerful influences in the direction of making most newspapers much less the personal utterances of their editors than nineteenth-century newspapers had been. Highly personalized journalism, possible only when the paper was small, was being replaced by a varied news program demanding an increased staff with specific talents. When newspapers became big business, it then became clear to so-called "managing editors" that if newspapers do not sell, they will fail. Great time and effort were put into researching what type of reporting would appeal to the public. The answer appeared to be summed up much later by Julius Chambers, managing editor of the *New York Evening World*, who, in discussing which newspapers succeed, stated: "In every case the successful American journal has been built on sensationalism."4 The term *sensationalism* was used to refer to the "detailed newspaper treatment of crimes, disasters, sex scandals and monstrosities" which stimulated emotional, often unhealthy, responses in the average reader.5 Although these issues had always aroused great curiosity in most people for untold generations, this is the first time that sensationalism was used as a regular, expected, and accepted method of reporting. This sensationalism, which became commonplace in the early 1900s, would have shocked the moralist of the just lapsed Victorian period. However, the new American of the twentieth century obviously did not find it shocking or repulsive. Pulitzer, Hearst, and other publishers realized that interest in crime and sex was universal. Soon newspapers were filled with melodramatic headlines and stories reported in a startling style appealing to raw human emotion, albeit occasionally pathologic and salacious.

Clearly, American newspaper readers were ready in January 1907 as the courtroom in Manhattan was prepared for the "trial of the century" to be treated to a new type of news coverage. This coverage was exciting, sentimental, prurient, mawkish, soppy—and tear-jerking. What better name to be applied to this new style of reporting than sob sister journalism.

But sob sister journalism was not destined to be a passing fad. Indeed this type of reportage laid the groundwork not only for the future careers of the "sob sisters" but for a vast array of reporters, authors, radio and television personalities, and movie stars. The four women journalists themselves went on to capitalize on their distinctive styles and continued to make use of the sob sister approach in most of their subsequent endeavors (see Chapter 7).

Beyond its impact on the productivity and style of these journalists, its effect on the entire American culture is undisputed. The very principles and stylistic manner used by the sob sisters can be seen in the development of any number of advice columns, gossip sheets, and movie scripts. Even courtroom reportage continued to make use of "sob sister" journalism as recently as the famous Dr. Sam Shepherd murder trial, where Dorothy Kilgallen and others stepped into the shoes of the pioneer "sob sisters." Nowhere is the unrelenting evolution of the sob sister approach more apparent than in the development of soap operas, which have become at the very least a cornerstone in American entertainment and perhaps have attained an important enough place in the American psyche to have a profound effect on the social, psychological, sexual, and even political life of the populace—especially women.

NOTES

1. Edward Wagenknecht, *American Profile: 1900–1910* (Amherst, Mass.: University of Massachusetts Press, 1982), p. 49.

2. Frank Mott, *American Journalism* (New York: Macmillan, 1950), p. 549.

3. Ibid., p. 547.

4. Ibid., p. 443.

5. Ibid., p. 442.

Chapter 7

Epilogue

WINIFRED BLACK

Born: October 14, 1863
Died: May 26, 1936

The body of Mrs. Winifred Black Bonfils lay in state in the rotunda of the San Francisco City Hall, placed there by decree of Mayor Angelo Rossi. Thousands of men, women, and children filed past the bier. Huge banks of flowers and wreaths filled the rotunda. Among the offerings were many little bouquets of garden flowers brought by child admirers.[1]

Annie Laurie's fame as a reporter and writer was worldwide. Her formula for reportorial success, which she gave freely to women reporters who asked for it, was:

The ideal newspaper women has the keen zest for life of a child, the cool courage of a man and the subtlety of a woman. A woman has a distinct advantage over a man in reporting, if she has sense enough to balance her qualities. Men always are good to women. At least I have found them so and I've been in some of the toughest places.[2]

Following the Thaw trial Black returned to her position with the *Denver Post* but remained for only three years. Her 1901 marriage to Charles Bonfils, managing editor of the *Kansas City Post*, was failing and she preferred "traveling around the world in pursuit of the news to staying home in Denver with her husband."[3]

In 1910 she traveled to England to report on the British suffragettes. This was an especially militant group who fought the police and protested the treatment of women by pouring acid in letter boxes.[4]

By 1915, Black, still using her *nom de plume* Annie Laurie, had become a San Francisco institution. She would attack anyone who stood in the way of her crusades. "Every time there was a hint of demolition of historic buildings, Black gave such loud shrieks of anguish in a public way that the matter was dropped cold."[5] After the Exposition of 1915, speculators tried to seize the site and tear down the Palace of Fine Arts, considered by many to be one of the most beautiful buildings in the world. Through her efforts societies and clubs were organized to fight the move.[6]

Black and her husband were reunited briefly in 1917, but soon separated. Black explained, "His paper was his sweetheart and his wife and his child and his smart outfit, it was his life and his heart's blood and the very soul of him."[7] The couple were never divorced.

She went to Europe in 1918 to study the effects of World War I and the rumored armistice on American soldiers. Her copy in the *San Francisco Examiner* warned families "that their returning sons and lovers would probably be different people from those whom they had bid good-bye several years earlier: older, sadder, less trustful, less full of hope."[8] Few of her stories appeared in the *Examiner*, because they were censored, a fact which incensed Black and resulted in several articles harshly berating the censors.[9] In 1918 she was called to Washington to chair the U.S. Garden Army committee, which entailed a campaign to encourage American children to plant Victory Gardens at home so that more foodstuffs could be shipped to soldiers overseas.[10]

One of the last articles Black wrote in her sob sister style was an obituary in 1919 of Phoebe Apperson Hearst, mother of William

Randolph Hearst. His confidence in Black made Hearst turn to her as the one woman he would allow to write his mother's obituary.[11] So adamant was he that he proclaimed if Black could not be found, only a straight news account could appear in the newspaper. Forty minutes before deadline the *Examiner* staff found Black aboard a ferry in San Francisco Bay, rushed her back to the office where she wrote a three-column feature article eulogizing Phoebe Hearst. Later, she wrote a 200-page memorial biography about her.[12]

She continued to write her regular "Annie Laurie" columns for the *San Francisco Examiner* and in 1931 traveled to Geneva for the League of Nations narcotics conference. She urged in her writing "international treaties of cooperation in fighting and controlling narcotic traffic."[13] Much of her writing during her last ten years was in support of stronger drug control, including a book entitled *Dope, the Story of the Living Dead.*[14]

Despite increasing complications of diabetes and arteriosclerosis, she continued to keep up a healthy working pace. By 1936, blinded as a result of her illnesses, she was confined to her bed. She continued writing weekly "about five articles for the Hearst syndicate and three 'Annie Laurie' columns for the *Examiner*."[15]

When she was dying, Hearst's solicitude toward her was like that of a brother. Every hour he sent her warm, encouraging messages designed to cheer her and make her feel his presence though he could not be with her at the moment.

A caller found her in tears, as she listened to one of these messages. They talked for a time of her work on the Hearst papers, of the happy time she had spent at San Simeon with the Chief. As death approached, her mind was full of this man who had so dominated her life, and, as the visitor prepared to leave, the woman whom millions had known as Annie Laurie waved with a peculiarly despairing gesture toward her house and what it contained. "It's all—all Hearst," she murmured. Black died at the age of seventy-three survived by her estranged husband.[16]

ELIZABETH MERIWETHER GILMER
(DOROTHY DIX)

Born: November 18, 1861
Died: December 16, 1951

Coverage of the Thaw-White trial won for Gilmer a new contract calling for $13,000 a year—the most money paid to any women journalist in the United States.[17] She was simultaneously writing her "Dorothy Dix Talks" column. As time went on Dix, though excellent at her craft, was getting tired of murder stories and felt her contribution in reporting these events did little more than boost newspaper circulation. Her advice column, on the other hand, was of help to people who needed help. Dix had a heavy sense of responsibility about her work. Over the years she grew so adept that she could absorb the contents of a letter "almost at a glance and make up her mind quickly on the issues raised."[18] Realizing that at the moment her correspondents were writing to her, they were undergoing a genuine emotional upheaval, she did not take their letters lightly.

Dorothy Dix was credited with an audience of 35 million readers and received from 100 to 2,000 letters a day. Her column was syndicated in 200 newspapers in the United States, Canada, England, the Philippines, Japan, China, South Africa, and Australia and was translated into Japanese and Spanish.[19]

In 1916 she left the Hearst group and signed a contract with the Wheeler Syndicate. This gave her an opportunity to quit writing the "tales of murder and mayhem" that she had been doing for sixteen years while with the *Journal*.[20] Publishing six times weekly, she devoted her time exclusively to "Dorothy Dix Talks." Half her column was devoted to printing actual letters from readers and half to her own sermonettes.[21]

Mrs. Gilmer felt that the letters kept her "in touch with the world's current point of view."[22] "Sometimes," she wrote, "I wonder what my correspondents would think if I answered their inquiries as I would have had to answer them forty years ago."[23]

She moved back to New Orleans and wrote from a spacious home overlooking Audubon Park in the Garden District of the city. Received as a celebrity, Dix became an active participant in the city's civic and social life.[24]

During this period George Gilmer was experiencing alternate bouts of melancholia and anger. He moved to Florida, and though she remained the sole support of the family, an extended separation ensued.

Dix remained with the Wheeler Syndicate until 1923, when she signed with the Ledger Syndicate and subsequently in 1942 wrote for the Bell Syndicate. She continued writing from her stone mansion in New Orleans furnished with antiques and objets d'art.[25] She "dined at a table taken from the palace of a Bonaparte under a chandelier that had dropped wax on the dandies of the Empire."[26]

Her biographer, Harnett T. Kane, writes, "by the mid-1920's, Dorothy Dix, sometimes to her own embarrassment, found herself much in the limelight . . . for the first time in her career an enterprising organization went to work to let America know what Miss Dix had to offer. It has been speculated that her popularity increased because the day of the speakeasy, bathtub gin, and flappers produced a need in the country for a certain affirmation, and turned—without understanding why—to her brand of practical advice."[27] She eventually earned upwards of $90,000 a year.[28]

Gilmer was also writing articles under her real name and being published regularly in Hearst magazines, chiefly *Good Housekeeping* and *Cosmopolitan*. Between 1910 and 1920 she wrote her "Mirandy" series of stories containing conversation of Mirandy with other black persons, expressing a brand of folk wisdom. These were a regular feature in *Good Housekeeping* and salable enough to be collected in two volumes in 1914 and 1925.[29]

Gilmer had a love of travel which she fulfilled on several trips to the Orient. The first trip took place in 1917 when she was still with the Wheeler Syndicate, and the second in 1923, which coincided with her switch to the Ledger Syndicate.[30] She recorded these travels in "My Trip Around the World," published by Penn

Publishing Company in 1924. Her tourist essays are models of
keen observation and humor and can still be read as guides to the
traveler.

Gilmer's life spanned great social changes. She was an early
advocate of the proposed nineteenth amendment (for women's
suffrage). From the turn of the century, she campaigned in her
columns for women's education and the right to employment.
Though she felt that mothers of young children should work only
out of necessity, she did advocate that all women should be trained
at some vocation.[31]

At age sixty-five Gilmer's most important book was published.
Entitled "Dorothy Dix—Her Book: Everyday Help for Everyday
People," it sold well enough to go into three printings.[32]

Its importance can be attributed in part to her philosophy of life:

> I have been through the depths of poverty and sickness. . . . I
> have known want and struggle and anxiety and despair. . . .
> As I look back upon my life I see it as a battlefield strewn
> with the wrecks of dead dreams and broken hopes and shat-
> tered illusions—a battle in which I always fought with the
> odds tremendously against me, and which has left me scarred
> and bruised and maimed and old before my time.
>
> But I have learned to live each day as it comes, and not to
> borrow trouble by dreading the morrow. It is the dark menace
> of the picture that makes cowards of us. I put that dread from
> me because experience has taught me that when the time
> comes that I so fear, the strength and wisdom to meet it will
> be given me.[33]

In June 1927 she received a Doctor of Letters degree from
Tulane University "in recognition of her contribution to the quality
of life in the United States." The following year New Orleans
celebrated "Dorothy Dix Day" so that "women of all sorts—factory workers, housewives, welfare officials and others could honor
her."[34]

At this point in her life when honors were coming, painful moments were coming as well. Overnight the problem of George Gilmer escalated. He had left Florida and was heading toward New Orleans with grim accusations and threats against his wife. His relatives met the train with a car and took him directly to an asylum, where he remained until his death in January 1929.[35]

Following her husband's death she continued dispensing her sage advice until 1949, when she conceded that she was unable to continue. A year later she suffered a stroke and was hospitalized for the last twenty-one months of her life. She died in the Touro Infirmary, New Orleans, at the age of ninety.[36]

NIXOLA GREELEY-SMITH

Born: April 5, 1880
Died: March 9, 1919

During the Thaw trial Nixola Greeley-Smith met Andrew Waters Ford, who later became the city editor of the *New York Evening Telegram*. During the trial their close association blossomed into friendship and romance.[37] The Fords were married on April 1, 1910, and moved to 130 West 57th Street, New York City.[38] The marriage was happy despite the fact that her love for newspaper work was so strong that she couldn't give up her job and become solely a housewife. She continued to work at the *New York Evening World*.

The *Evening World* paid her $80 a week, and she was allowed to pick her own assignments. She was considered by many to be the first women to obtain and write really intelligent interviews with prominent men and women. In fact, her obituary states, "there is almost no man or woman of note in this country and almost no distinguished European visitor who has not spoken in her column of the *Evening World* through the brilliantly accurate interpretation of Nixola Greeley-Smith."[39]

Recognizing her capabilities, Sam Hughes of the Newspaper Enterprise Association, headquartered in the same building as the

World, offered her a two-year contract at $7,000 a year which, against her better judgment, she accepted.[40]

The job did not prove satisfactory. Unable to choose her assignments, she considered those she was handed "ridiculous stunts beneath the dignity of an established newswoman."[41] She resigned after two years at the completion of her contract and returned to the *Evening World*, where she felt at home though she continued to receive job offers from as far away as England. William Randolph Hearst made many offers but she turned them all down.[42]

Although her strength was in the personal interview, she often did straight news assignments. In 1914 she covered the sinking of the *Empress of Ireland* when 954 lives were lost.[43] She also continued to cover other famous trials.

It was Nixola who gave Theda Bara her professional name. The actress, who was born Dora Goodman, explained during an interview that she must have a new name. After considerable thought Nixola picked Theda Bara since it suited the actress's exotic type. "Bara" is "Arab" spelled backwards.[44]

Greeley-Smith was one of the most valued and hard-working members of the Publicity Section of the New York State Women's Suffrage Party.[45] She was in a theater when she heard that the vote had been won for women in New York State. She wept with joy. "This is the greatest day of my life," she said.[46]

She died in New York Hospital at age thirty-eight following an operation for acute appendicitis.[47] Margaret Mooers Marshall, who knew her well, wrote her impression of Greeley-Smith as a special tribute in her obituary.

"Write me, then, as one who loved her fellow-women"—that is what Nixola Greeley-Smith would have said of her today. For she was not merely a distinguished woman writer. She was a woman's writer, who frankly, fearlessly, lovingly sought to interpret and express her own sex—for her own sex—and, after that for the men of understanding to whom her wit and sanity made inevitable appeal.

But it was women who interested her, women whose tenderness she honored, women whose intelligence she upheld, women whose future was the faith she championed with all the resources of a brilliantly logical mind, and incandescent wit, a crystalline literary style and passionate loyalty.

She was a suffragist long before suffrage became fashionable. She was a believer in economic independence for women, married and unmarried, since she saw in this the surest lever for lifting the world's greatest injustice. She so reverenced the long labor and self sacrifice of mothers that she would have had the state give them pensions it gives to its other heroes. Her eighteen years on the staff of the *Evening World* were years of service to women.

She had rare understanding and sympathy for the problems of the woman who works for a wage. She touched with penetrating intelligence the hearts of restless wives. Yet she never lost her fresh, happy comprehension of the beauty of a girl's star-crowned romantic love.

Nor was her preoccupation with women confined to theory. Those near her will not soon forget her generous appreciations, her quick helpful friendliness, her honor and her charm. Women she barely knew, unknown, suffering women who wrote to her, never appealed in vain for comfort she could give.

In the death of Nixola Greeley-Smith American womanhood is bereft. As its ambassador, as well as out of deep personal grief, I say to a great woman writer and friend, "Hail—and farewell!"[48]

ADA PATTERSON

Born: Unknown
Died: June 26, 1939

Ada Patterson's work on the Thaw case was "penetrating and adroit" due to her shrewd knowledge of human reactions.[49] She had little time to rest after the second Thaw trial ended before she was assigned to the next murder trial she was to cover for the *New York American*. On August 18, 1908, Major Peter C. Haines shot and killed W. E. Annis, a magazine publisher and the lover of Haines's beautiful wife Claudia Libbey Haines.[50]

While on assignment in the Philippines, Haines received word from his brother, Thorton Jenkins Haines, that Claudia was constantly in the company of Annis. The major hurried home and confronted his wife. Following her confession he brought suit for divorce. Two months later Haines chose the site of the Bayside Yacht Club on Long Island to shoot Annis as he emerged from the water.

Mrs. Haines retreated to her mother's home in Boston. Ada Patterson went in pursuit. By using the name of a friend of Mr. Annis, she was allowed to see Mrs. Haines and was the only reporter to secure an interview.

During the interview Mrs. Haines, seemingly forgetting that she was talking to a journalist, condemned her husband and stood by her lover, all the time denigrating love and marriage. Patterson printed the story intellectually and compassionately.[51]

But her best reportorial work was done at the trial of Charles Becker, the police lieutenant, who was electrocuted in 1912 for the murder of Herman Rosenthal. She was the first reporter to interview Mrs. Lillian Rosenthal after the murder took place. She managed to get past guards protecting Mrs. Rosenthal from reporters, by getting a letter from Charles S. Whitman, district attorney of New York at the time.[52]

The case moved slowly and there were the usual appeals. Three years later a date of execution was set.

Miss Patterson went to Mrs. Rosenthal.

"Where are you going to be on the night of the execution?" she asked.

"I think the only thing to do is hide."

"Well, come and hide with me."

For two days and nights, while the press was hunting for Mrs. Rosenthal she was hiding in Ada Patterson's apartment.

On the night of the execution they kept vigil together. Mrs. Rosenthal was bitter and the women sat up all night while she poured out her wrath in Miss Patterson's ears.[53]

In 1923 Patterson resigned to devote her time to magazine work, writing for *Screenland, America, Psychology, Ladies Home Journal, Saturday Evening Post, Harper's Bazaar,* and *Liberty* magazines. She wrote inspirational and health articles and dramatic features.[54]

Miss Patterson continued covering murder trials as well as providing feature writing for the *New York American.* Her ability to get people to talk when other reporters failed led Arthur Brisbane to say: "When no one else can get a thing we send Ada Patterson after it."[55]

She continued this work until she retired to a hotel in Sarasota, Florida, two years before her death in 1939.[56]

STANFORD WHITE

Born: November 9, 1853
Died: June 25, 1906

Following the murder most of Stanford White's "inner circle" left the country for extensive travels on the continent. With the exception of Richard Harding Davis, they were unavailable for comment in support of their former colleague and friend. They were unavailable to refute claims by members of the press and others that White was a voluptuary and pervert whose death was due to the easy standard of morals he had set up for himself.[57]

According to the *Evening Journal* many of White's friends sought by the investigators fled "before the threatened scandal and exposure. Those who remained were dreading the sensational revelations which were expected to follow the investigation."[58]

Stanford White emerged as a satyr leading a life that might have occurred in the "Neronic period of the Roman empire."[59] Dorothy Dix wrote, "His name became a hissing in the mouths of men when it became known the manner of life he had led."[60] White, it was said, paid ardent devotion to a "score of beautiful girls still in their teens. He would dress them in costly raiment, lavish them with expensive jewels and provide money for their whims."[61]

White had three hideaway spots to take his girls: his studio in the tower of Madison Square Garden, his apartment at 122 East 22nd Street, and a *pied à terre* at 22 West Twenty-fourth Street.[62] Reports claimed that White, often with another gentleman as co-host, would invite "young girls of surpassing beauty and charm of person, but socially obscure" to one of these spots where a banquet would be served and unlimited quantities of champagne imbibed.[63]

Reporters described White as the "archetype of a species sadly common in the cities of the United States and indigenous to New York. He was wealthy. He had business standing of a high order. His social prominence was equal to his eminence in the professional world."[64]

The type of man with whom White was identified was considered a menace to the young, unsophisticated girl to whom "the world is a fairyland and every man a Prince Charming."[65] These girls wanted to go on the stage, and they believed that men like Stanford White were the key to unlock the stage door to them. "Come up and see my etchings" became a popular wisecrack after this case, from one of Stanford White's indirect invitations when settling on a new girl in the chorus.[66]

The girls, it was reported, claimed that "Mr. White is so kind." Afterward, if they were wise, they would say nothing at all. "The man did all the talking, for he lacked that essential of a gentleman suggested by the Prince of Wales—silence. It was in his boasting, his coarse jests, his pomp of vice that he showed his satiric side."[67] It was reported that on several occasions White did secure positions for the girls, usually in the chorus of a musical comedy from which they found themselves unemployed once the show left New York.

Many reporters described the kind of life that White led behind the closed doors of his alleged studios as a revelation of crimes committed in the name of art. They told tales of youthful models, chorus girls, and shop girls who would pose for their hosts. The hosts would get out palette and brush and paint their guests "as lonely creatures, as Aphrodite or wood nymphs."[68] When details of these revels were revealed, the public was shocked, flabbergasted, and fascinated. Everyone's imagination embellished the story.

Probably the most shocking story was the one that Susie Johnson, a fifteen-year-old blond, blue-eyed photographer's model, confided to a friend. Susie, one of seven children, was raised on the top floor of a tenement on Eighth Avenue. There she lived with her sisters and brothers and a father who was usually drunk and often neglected to bring him his weekly wage. Her father was taken sick, and at age eleven Susie went to work at a braid factory. The work was exhausting, and after three years, Susie was forced, due to ill health, to search for other employment.

"I had to get something light to do, so my mother took me to Mr. Clark, the artist, in response to his advertisement for a model." This was the beginning of a career that paid a dollar an hour and which she thought was easy work. The artists liked her. They called her "The Little Sister of the Studios."[69]

In 1895 one of the artists offered Susie $50 to be the "Girl in the Pie" at a dinner given by Jim Brease, in his studio at No. 5 East Sixteenth Street.[70] This was a tempting sum, and with her mother's consent she began making preparations for the dinner. Out of the rates paid her for extra posing her mother bought fabric and made a black gauze robe, through which her slim arms and ankles were exposed.

On the night of the $350-a-plate banquet Susie was placed in an iron vessel with twenty-four canaries in a cage that she held in her hand. A crust with air holes in it had been placed over the vessel, and when the banjoists struck up the tune "Four and Twenty Blackbirds Baked in a Pie," she burst through the crust, opened the cage, so that the birds would fly out, and found herself being stared at by thirty men and two women, also models.

Susie was lifted from the pie to a seat on the table where she was toasted and encouraged by Stanford White to drink champagne until the early hours of the morning. White then took Susie in her "stupefied condition" to his studio apartment on Twenty-fourth Street. Susie remained in White's affections for two years, when he sent her to Europe to be educated for the stage. After three months her allowance stopped, and she took the first steamer home. To her distress White would have nothing further to do with her.

Penniless, she obtained a position as governess for two children in Brooklyn. For two years she lived in this peaceful environment. She married, but was divorced when her husband learned of her past at the Brease studio dinner and left her.

Repulsed by the friends to whom she had applied for help and ashamed to go back to the studios, Susie Johnson on January 14, 1903, took her life. She was buried in Potter's Field.[71]

Even White's wife of many years appeared to have deserted him. After the funeral, Mrs. White went to Europe and not once did she raise her voice in defense of her husband. Ada Patterson wrote of Mrs. White's silence:

A man's desserts are poor indeed when his wife or widow can say not for him. For every scoundrel there is always a romantic sacrificial defender, who shuts her eyes to all evil in him and strikes out aimlessly and futilely in every direction in his defense. This defender is usually of his own home, almost always is his wife or widow. Sentimentalists speak of the beauty of her blind faith. But at the root of it is an intense, if unwise, loyalty, and loyalty in almost any guise is admirable. If a man have any Godlikeness in him he is enshrined in his own home. If he is not there enshrined we men safely conclude that there is much of the opposite quality in him. The Sphinx has not been more mute in his defense than she.[72]

White's lone public defender was not one of his inner circle, but Richard Harding Davis, considered to be the "beau ideal of foreign correspondents" and known as an "apostle of cleanness and wholesomeness."[73] In an article published in *Collier's* magazine on August 4, 1906, Davis wrote about his fifteen-year acquaintance with White:

> One who is permitted to write a few true words about a man who never spoke an unkind one, resents the fact that before he can try to tell what Stanford White was, he must first tell what Stanford White was not. . . . Since his death White has been described as a satyr. To answer this by saying that he was a great architect is not to answer it at all. . . . What is more important is that he was a most kind-hearted, most considerate, gentle and manly man, who could no more have done the things attributed to him than he could have roasted a baby on the spit. Big in mind and body, he was incapable of little meannesses. He admired a beautiful woman as he admired every other beautiful thing that God has given us; and his delight over one was as keen, as boyish, as grateful as over any of the others. Described as a voluptuary, his greatest pleasure was to stand all day waist deep in the rapids of a Canadian river and fight it out with the salmon.[74]

HARRY KENDALL THAW

Born: February 1, 1871
Died: February 22, 1947

Mrs. William Thaw continued her legal efforts. In 1909, she wrote an impassioned, rambling pamphlet entitled *The Secret Unveiled*, in which she described her son as "an average young man with a chivalrous nature" who was being persecuted by a cabal of Stanford White's influential friends.[75]

From his new address at the Asylum for the Criminal Insane at Matteawan Thaw was demanding the right to another jury trial to determine his sanity. He carried the question to the United States Supreme Court, which ruled against him in December 1909.[76]

The hearing had featured the testimony of Mrs. Susan Merrill, former proprietor of a boarding house in New York. Mrs. Merrill thought she was renting Thaw rooms for the purpose of training girls for the stage. In reality, she testified, he used the rooms for sadistic whippings of girls, whose testimony he had silenced at a price of $40,000.[77]

At his next sanity hearing in June 1912, Evelyn testified against her husband, talking of threats he made to kill her as soon as he became a free man. He was once again returned to Matteawan.[78]

One year and two months later on August 17, 1913, newspapers brought readers the most sensational headlines since the night Thaw murdered Stanford White. According to the *New York Times*, about 7:30 on Sunday morning, Thaw opened the outer door of the hospital storeroom, where he worked as an assistant to the store-keeper, and walked into the asylum yard where he often took exercise. At the same moment a milkman's cart approached. When the gate was opened to allow the cart to enter the asylum grounds, Thaw exited through the open gate and leaped into a black limousine waiting on the other side of the road.

Thaw boarded a train and headed for Canada. Upon his arrival at Sherbrooke, Quebec, Thaw was arrested. The legalities were argued by Thaw's Canadian lawyers and an American delegation headed by Jerome.[79] During his stay in Canada, Thaw was becoming a celebrity and hero. "He would drive through the streets in an open carriage, waving with his hat to the crowds that called after him, 'Hurray for British fair play!' In fact Canadian feeling ran so strongly in favor of Thaw and opposed to American persecution" that one day Jerome found himself under arrest on a "trumped up" charge of gambling.[80]

On September 10, the Minister of Justice yielded to American pressure and ordered Thaw deported from Canada. He was taken, as a federal prisoner, to Concord, New Hampshire, where again he was cheered by crowds of sympathizers, and his fight against extradition to New York became a legal battleground. A year later, in December 1914, Thaw, by order of the United States Supreme Court, was returned to New York State.

Back in the Tombs, the prison in which he resided during the first two trials, Thaw settled down to a long trial in which a large percentage of the "evidence presented at his two trials for murder was recapitulated."[81]

On July 16, 1915, Harry Kendall Thaw was declared sane and acquitted of all charges. The verdict brought violent opposition. A portion of the editorial in the *New York Sun* entitled "How to be a Hero" read:

At length the long, ignominious drama is ended. The paranoiac walks forth free, declared sane by a jury of his intelligent fellow-citizens; and he becomes, as he had previously become even in sober New Hampshire, a conquering hero, the idol of "the populace." Cheering crowds crush around him. Women weep over him. Men esteem it an honor to shake the hand crimson with the blood of Stanford White. Washington or Lincoln could not be more deified than this murderer with the price.[82]

For a year and a half Thaw lived inconspicuously. Another Thaw scandal hit the headlines on January 9, 1917. He was indicted for the kidnapping and brutal whipping of a nineteen-year-old Kansas City youth, Frederick Gump, Jr. Thaw had met Gump in December 1915 at an ice cream parlor in Long Beach, California, where the boy's family was staying during his father's recuperation from a long illness. Thaw offered young Gump fifty dollars a month plus expenses either to take a job at the Highland Iron Works of Pittsburgh or to enroll as a student in the Carnegie Institute of Technology. The offer was so attractive that Gump was advised by his father to accept this chance at an education.[83]

Thaw arranged to met Gump at the McAlpin Hotel in New York to discuss final arrangements. The boy was to stay in the large suite Thaw occupied at the hotel. Shortly after Gump retired, Thaw reportedly "opened the door, switched on the light, and with a short whip proceeded to flog his victim almost into unconsciousness."[84]

The boy escaped, returned to Kansas City, and informed his parents of his experience. Thaw in the meantime had returned to Pittsburgh. In order to avoid his extradition to New York and another sensational trial, Mrs. William Thaw appealed to the courts of the State of Pennsylvania "to help a mother protect her son from infirmities" and urged the state to judge Thaw insane. Two months later a commission on lunacy committed him to the mental ward of the Pennsylvania State Hospital in Philadelphia.[85] While in the hospital Thaw wrote a "disjointed, incoherent autobiography entitled *The Traitor* which he published in 1926 at his own expense." In January 1924 a jury again found Thaw sane and he was released from the State Hospital.[86]

He continued to make headlines. In 1927 he was sued by a night club hostess named Marci Estardus, who claimed he had beaten her up at a party in his New York apartment on January 1, 1927. In the spring of 1931 after a third trial she was awarded $16,000.[87]

Six years later he was sued by Paul Jaeck, a hotel head waiter, assaulted by Thaw following a champagne party when he presented Thaw with the check. He was awarded $2,200.[88]

This seems to be the end of Thaw's craving for publicity. He settled down to the quietude of old age and on February 21, 1947, at the age of seventy-six, he suffered a heart attack in Miami, where he had rented a home on North Bay Road. He died the next day and was buried in the family plot in Allegheny Cemetery in Pittsburgh.[89]

EVELYN NESBIT THAW

Born: December 25, 1886
Died: January 17, 1967

Thinking she had a clear understanding with Mother Thaw and her lawyer, Evelyn assumed she would again testify in Thaw's defense and as soon as the second trial was over, begin divorce proceedings. The promised settlement was $1 million. Unknown to Evelyn, Mother Thaw had been collecting a dossier on her. It included details of several affairs, dinners, and trips with male acquaintances.

Following the verdict of insanity and Harry's commitment to Matteawan, Evelyn filed for an annulment claiming Harry Thaw was insane at the time of their marriage. Evelyn soon discovered that an annulment denied her claim to his estate, and since Harry was declared of "unsound mind," any divorce settlement would be controlled by his mother. Mother Thaw dropped the offered price from $1 million to $25,000, considering this sum only because Evelyn's testimony might be needed in future sanity hearings. Evelyn insisted she be paid in advance. Quickly going through her advance Evelyn moved from their home on Park Avenue to the cheap Prince George Hotel on Twenty-eighth Street.[90]

Evelyn was unable to secure work; "notoriety had closed every avenue." Denying Evelyn support, Harry's mother thought Evelyn would "land in the gutter, and thereby gain public sympathy for her son."[91]

Harry refused to pay any outstanding bills, stating that his creditors would have to get together and demand his release so that he could get out and pay them. Instead they sued Evelyn. Every time she left her apartment, she was met by process servers accosting her with papers.[92] A lover of reptiles, Evelyn, for her twenty-fourth birthday, was presented with a six-foot Florida king snake by her good friend Dr. Raymond Ditmars, curator at the Bronx Zoo.[93] One day, by chance, she discovered the "cure" for process servers. "Descending the stairs from my studio apartment with Tara [the king snake] wound around my arm, I espied three process servers puffing and panting up the stairs. They stopped when they saw me a few paces above them, and mopped their brows. Then their eyes discerned Tara, who was restlessly unwinding a few coils, his head arched upward like a question-mark and swaying from side to side. The first man let out a wild yell and fell backwards unbalancing the two others. Head over heels they tumbled down the stairs and dashed down the street. I was served with no more writs and saw no more bill-collectors."[94]

After persuasion from several friends, Harry consented to give Evelyn seventy-five dollars a month for living expenses. Her visits to Matteawan, which had stopped with the cessation of support, resumed. On one of these visits to his private apartment at Matteawan Evelyn became pregnant. With a desire to give the child a "fair start in life" Evelyn thought an extended visit to Europe was needed. Accompanied by a friend to give moral support, she visited Matteawan for the purpose of informing Thaw of his paternity and requesting funding for her journey. She began by asking Harry to send her to Europe. His furious refusal angered Evelyn who lost her temper, walked out, and never informed Thaw of the impending birth.

Deciding to take her life's direction into her own hands, she developed "unprecedented courage and determination."[95] Robert Collier, son of the publisher of *Collier's* weekly, had tried in 1901 to convince Evelyn she was wasting her time on the stage and proposed to send her to art school in Paris. At the time she refused his offer, to which he replied "any time you change your mind, I'll be only too glad to send you abroad. No strings attached to the offer."[96]

She approached Collier, who was delighted to send her to Europe, albeit not to attend art school as was his original offer, but so that she could be "independent of Thaw and his family and enjoy the peace of mind necessary during the prenatal period."[97] Concerned that she should not be alone in her "condition," he arranged for Evelyn to be accompanied by her good friend from Floradora days, Lillian Spencer.[98] On October 25, 1910, Russell William Thaw, weighing eight pounds at birth, was born in Berlin. Two weeks later Evelyn and son returned to New York.

Upon her return Evelyn moved to an apartment with Jack Francis, newspaperman and good friend, who had been summoned, on short notice, to replace Lillian Spencer as Evelyn's European companion. Lillian suddenly had to return to New York for rehearsal of a play in which she was to star.

Her living arrangements were short-lived. Jack became insanely jealous and the two began to argue. Jack betrayed Evelyn's trust and sold her story to the *New York Herald*. It ran under the title "Evelyn Nesbit Thaw's Secret Baby," and Francis received seventy-five dollars for the scoop.[99]

Evelyn was destitute. When her allowance from Thaw was stopped, she had to sell everything—pictures, rugs, jewelry—everything. She had to find a means to earn a living and support herself and her son, Russell.

The course of Evelyn's life was soon to take an abrupt change. The bright light in her poverty struck with an invitation to a party of Flo Ziegfield's. There she met a Canadian lawyer who fell in love with her. He convinced her to join him, accompanied by her baby and friend Lillian Spencer, on a six-month business trip to Europe.

They sailed together for Paris aboard the *Olympia* in May 1913. Aboard ship Evelyn met H. B. Marinelli, an international theatrical agent. Before the boat docked in France, Evelyn had secured a contract to appear at the London Hippodrome in *Hello Ragtime*.[100]

The play opened to rave reviews. Oscar Hammerstein saw the play and offered Evelyn $3,500 a week to open in New York. She agreed. The Victoria Theatre was packed for every show. Never in the annals of vaudeville had attendance records been equaled, not even by Sarah Bernhardt when she appeared in vaudeville.[101] Her agent booked her for a tour. She traveled with her dance partner Jack Clifford across the country doing two shows a day. She broke records in every city including taking in $37,500 in one week in Chicago.

Evelyn told a reporter for the *Boston Herald*, "I thank God I don't need to ask him for money any more. Nothing was ever sweeter in my whole life than earning my own living and being independent of the Thaws and the Thaws' money."[102]

Evelyn's success "nettled" Mother Thaw, who, without success, tried to stop Evelyn's next appearance, claiming that ragtime dances were "immoral and immodest." In reply, as though to refute her charge, the Pittsburgh audience gave Evelyn a fifteen-minute standing ovation.[103]

Evelyn was on the road in 1915 when she was served with divorce papers by a recently declared sane Harry Thaw. Free, she married her dance partner Jack Clifford, and they continued to work the town as husband and wife until 1919. Then, at the urging of the United Booking Office, Evelyn was encouraged to engage a new partner, one not as limited to acrobatics. The partnership dissolved, and their marriage soon began to suffer. The marriage ended in divorce a few years later with Evelyn asserting that Clifford had lived on $100,000 of her money from 1916 to 1918.[104] In the early 1920s Evelyn developed "facial neuralgia." With the help of a ex-Follies girlfriend, she found relief through morphine injections. She soon became addicted and attempted withdrawal at a "milk farm" in New Jersey. She spent six weeks eating no food and only drinking rich, real, natural milk all day long.[105] She managed to reduce her drug requirement to a small dose but could never "dislodge the craving altogether."[106]

In 1921 Evelyn briefly attempted to manage a tearoom on West Fifty-seventh Street in New York.[107] Then she again returned to the stage, appearing in night clubs in Atlantic City and Chicago, where one of the novelties of the time was the appearance by the former Mrs. Harry Thaw singing such songs as "I'm a Broad Minded Broad from Broadway."[108]

At this time she made her first attempt at suicide by drinking Lysol following eviction for nonpayment of rent. She recovered and returned to Atlantic City, where Thaw visited her and promised to support her and Russell, the son he finally acknowledged fathering. Whatever the reason, nothing came of the apparent reconciliation.[109]

Still addicted to drugs, Evelyn failed to dispel her feelings of "heavy inertia." In 1924, at thirty-nine years of age, she weighed less than one hundred pounds and longed for her lost health and looks.

Once again, in the face of disaster, her luck changed. Harry Katz, proprietor of an Atlantic City night club, offered Evelyn one-half of the cover charge receipts and free hotel accommodations to headline in his establishment. She accepted the offer, abandoned her heroin habit, and with the proper diet and exercise, soon began regaining her health and beauty.

Following a dispute with Katz, Evelyn opened her own club, but its success was short-lived when her backers, during the time of prohibition, could not arrange the necessary payoff to the Treasury men.

Two years later she turned up inexplicably in a Yiddish drama in Atlantic City. In 1928 she drank a heavy dose of disinfectant in an unsuccessful attempt to take her life after a New Year's Eve celebration.

Following the second attempt at suicide Evelyn again took to the road, singing in seedy night clubs from Biloxi, Mississippi, to Panama City, Panama. In 1931 she returned to New York City in poor health suffering from a kidney ailment. She was placed in the Park West Sanitorium and in nine weeks was on her way to recovery.[110]

Evelyn wrote the story of her life entitled *Prodigal Days: The Untold Story* and had it published in 1934. Following the publication of her book she moved to California where she pursued a career as a sculpture and art instructor.[111] She lived in a rooming house in Hollywood for a while after World War II, practically penniless and apparently supported by her son Russell William Thaw.[112]

In 1955 she collaborated as writer and technical consultant for the Technicolor movie "The Girl in the Red Velvet Swing" that purported to be the story of her life. The movie starred Ray Milland as Stanford White, Farley Granger as Harry K. Thaw, and Joan Collins as Evelyn.[113] Evelyn received $30,000 for her efforts, which went for medical treatment following a cerebral stroke on June 9, 1956.[114]

Early in the 1960s she was moved to a nursing home. She died in Hollywood on January 17, 1967, at the age of eighty-one, all too aware that her life had really ended that night sixty years earlier at the roof garden. In her last interview Evelyn Nesbit Thaw sadly revealed, "Stanford White was the only man I ever loved."[115]

NOTES

1. *New York Evening Journal*, 27 May 1936.

2. Ishbel Ross, *Ladies of the Press: The Story of Women in Journalism by an Insider* (New York: Harper and Bros., 1936), p. 67.

3. *Dictionary of Literary Biography*, vol. 5 (Detroit, Mich.: Gale Research Company, 1983), p. 18.

4. Ibid., p. 17.

5. Ross, *Ladies of the Press*, p. 66.

6. Madelon Golden Schlipp and Sharon M. Murphy, *Great Women of the Press* (Carbondale: Southern Illinois University Press, 1983), p. 148.

7. *Dictionary of Literary Biography*, p. 25.

8. Schlipp, *Great Women of the Press*, p. 156.

9. *Dictionary of Literary Biography*, p. 25.

10. Schlipp, *Great Women of the Press*, p. 156.

11. Ross, *Ladies of the Press*, p. 153.

12. *Dictionary of Literary Biography*, p. 25.

13. Schlipp, *Great Women of the Press*, p. 157.

14. Ibid.

15. *Dictionary of Literary Biography*, p. 25.

16. Ibid.

17. Ibid., p. 116.

18. Ross, *Ladies of the Press*, p. 78.

19. Ibid., p. 75.

20. Schlipp, *Great Women of the Press*, p. 119.

21. Ibid., p. 117.

22. John E. Drewry, *Post Biographies of Famous Reporters* (Athens: University of Georgia Press, 1942), p. 45.

23. Ibid.

24. Schlipp, *Great Women of the Press*, p. 117.

25. Ibid., p. 119.

26. Ross, *Ladies of the Press*, p. 75.

27. Harnett T. Kane and Ella Bentley Arthur, *Dear Dorothy Dix* (New York: Doubleday and Company, 1952), p. 232.

28. Schlipp, *Great Women of the Press*, p. 119.

29. *Dictionary of Literary Biography*, p. 29.

30. Ibid.

31. Schlipp, *Great Women of the Press*, p. 118.

32. *Dictionary of Literary Biography*, p. 29.

33. Kane, *Dear Dorothy Dix*, p. 7.

34. Ibid., p. 244.

35. Ibid., p. 235.

36. Schlipp, *Great Women of the Press*, p. 119.

37. John W. Jakes, *Great Women Reporters* (New York: G. P. Putnam's Sons, 1969), p. 87.

38. *New York Evening World*, 10 March 1919.

39. Ibid.

40. Jakes, *Great Women Reporters*, p. 87.

41. Ibid.

42. Ibid., p. 88.

43. Ibid., p. 89.

44. Ross, *Ladies of the Press*, p. 92.

45. *New York Evening World*, 10 March 1919.

46. Ross, *Ladies of the Press*, p. 92.

47. *New York Evening World*, 3 October 1919.

48. Ibid.

49. Ross, *Ladies of the Press*, p. 67.

50. *New York Times*, 16 August 1908.

51. Ross, *Ladies of the Press*, p. 72.

52. Ibid., p. 70.

53. Ibid.

54. *New York Evening Journal and American*, 27 June 1939.

55. *Who Was Who Among North American Authors* (Detroit, Mich.: Gale Research Company, 1976), p. 1123.

56. *Sarasota Journal*, 27 June 1939.

57. *Vanity Fair Magazine*, 13 July 1906.

58. *New York Evening Journal*, 6 July 1906.

59. *Cincinnati Enquirer*, 27 June 1906.

60. *New York Evening Journal*, 23 January 1907.

61. *Cincinnati Enquirer*, 27 June 1906.

62. Charles C. Baldwin, *Stanford White* (New York: Dodd Mead, 1931), p. 22.

63. *Cincinnati Enquirer*, 27 June 1906.

64. *New York American*, 14 August 1906.

65. Ibid.

66. Baldwin, *Stanford White*, p. 28.

67. *New York American*, 14 August 1906.

68. *Cincinnati Enquirer*, 27 June 1906.

69. *New York Evening World*, 18 February 1907.

70. *New York Journal*, 18 February 1907.

71. Ibid.

72. *New York Evening Journal*, 2 February 1907.

73. John Tebbel, *The Compact History of the American Newspaper* (New York: Hawthorne Books, 1952), p. 187; Langford, *The Murder of Stanford White*, p. 44.

74. Langford, *The Murder of Stanford White*, p. 45.

75. Mrs. William Thaw, *The Secret Unveiled* (New York: A Pamphlet, 1909)

76. Langford, *The Murder of Stanford White*, p. 246.

77. Ibid.

78. Ibid.

79. *New York Times*, 17 June 1913.

80. Langford, *The Murder of Stanford White*, p. 251.

81. Ibid., p. 252.

82. *New York Sun*, 16 July 1915.

83. Langford, *The Murder of Stanford White*, p. 254.

84. Ibid.

85. Ibid., p. 255.

86. Ibid., pp. 256–257.

87. Ibid., p. 260.

88. Ibid.

89. *New York Times*, 23 February 1947.

90. Michael McDonald Mooney, *Evelyn Nesbit and Stanford White* (New York: William Morrow, 1976), p. 294.

91. Evelyn Nesbit, *Prodigal Days* (New York: Julian Messner, 1934), p. 205.

92. Ibid., p. 209.

93. Ibid., p. 219.

94. Ibid., p. 224.

95. Ibid., p. 219.

96. Ibid.

97. Ibid.

98. Ibid., p. 220.

99. Mooney, *Evelyn Nesbit and Stanford White*, p. 287.

100. Nesbit, *Prodigal Days*, p. 242.

101. Ibid., p. 244.

102. *Boston Herald*, 24 August 1913.

103. Nesbit, *Prodigal Days*, p. 247.

104. *New York Times*, 17 January 1967.

105. Nesbit, *Prodigal Days*, p. 259.

106. Ibid., p. 260.

107. Langford, *The Murder of Stanford White*, p. 257.

108. Ibid.

109. Ibid., p. 258.

110. Nesbit, *Prodigal Days*, p. 285.

111. *New York Times*, 19 January 1967.
112. Mooney, *Evelyn Nesbit and Stanford White*, p. 218.
113. Ibid., p. 298.
114. *New York Times*, 9 June 1956.
115. *American Weekly*, 14 September 1955.

Selected Bibliography

Addams, Jane. *Twenty Years at Hull House*. New York: Macmillan, 1910.

American Weekely, September 14, 1955.

Baldwin, Charles C. *Stanford White*. New York: Dodd, Mead and Co., 1931.

Baral, Robert. *Turn West on 23rd*. New York: Fleet Publishing Corporation, 1965.

Baxandall, Rosalyn, Gordon, Linda, and Reverdy, Susan. *America's Working Women*. New York: Random House, 1976.

Bleyer, William Grosvenor. *Main Currents in the History of American Journalism*. Boston: Houghton Mifflin, 1927.

Boston Herald. August 24, 1913.

Bremer, Robert H. *From the Depths: The Discovery of Poverty in the United States*. New York: New York University Press, 1972.

Brownlee, W. Elliott, and Brownlee, Mary. *Women and the Economy, a Documentary History: 1675-1929*. New Haven, Conn.: Yale University Press, 1976.

Cincinnati Enquirer. June 27, 1906.

Cochran, Thomas, and Milke, William. *The Age of Enterprise, A Social History of Industrial America*. New York: The Macmillan Co., 1942.

Collins, Frederick. *Glamorous Sinners*. New York: Ray Long and Richard R. Smith, Inc., 1932.

Davis, Allen F., and Woodman, Harold D. *Conflict and Consensus in Modern American History*, 6th ed., Lexington, Mass.: D. C. Heath and Co., 1984.

Dictionary of Literary Biography. Detroit, Mich.: Gale Research Company, 1983.

Doctorow, E. L. *Ragtime*. New York: Bantam Books, 1975.

Drewry, John E. *Post Biographies of Famous Journalists*. Athens: The University of Georgia Press, 1942.

Eisenstein, Sarah. *Give Us Bread but Give Us Roses*. London: Routledge and Kegan Paul, 1983.

Evans, Eli. *The Provincials*. New York: Atheneum, 1973.

Flynn, Elizabeth Gurley. *I Speak My Own Piece: Autobiography of the Rebel Girl*. New York: Masses and Mainstream, 1955.

Friedman, Jean E., and Shade, William G. *Our American Sisters: Women in American Life and Thought*. Lexington, Mass.: D. C. Heath and Company, 1982.

Gilman, Charlotte Perkins. *The Living of Charlotte Perkins Gilman: an Autobiography*. New York: Arno Press, 1972.

Gilman, Charlotte Perkins. *Women and Economics*. New York: Source Book Press, 1970.

Gould, Lewis. *The Progressive Era*. New York: Syracuse University Press, 1974.

Hammack, David. *Power and Society: Greater New York at the Turn of the Century*. New York: Russell Sage Foundation, 1982.

Handlin, Oscar. *The Uprooted*. Boston: Little, Brown, 1973.

Hymowitz, Carol, and Weissman, Michaele. *A History of Women in America*. New York: Bantam Books, Inc., 1978.

Irwin, Inez Haynes. *Angels and Amazons: A Hundred Years of American Women*. Garden City, N.Y.: Doubleday, Doran and Company, Inc., 1933.

Jakes, John W. *Great Women Reporters*. New York: G. P. Putnam's Sons, 1969.

Kane, Harnett T., with Arthur, Ella Bentley. *Dear Dorothy Dix: The Story of a Compassionate Woman*. New York: Doubleday and Co., 1952.

Kobre, Sidney. *Development of American Journalism*. Dubuque, Iowa: W. C. Brown and Co., 1969.

Kobre, Sidney. *The Yellow Press and Gilded Age Journalism*. Talahassee, Fla.: Florida State University, 1964.

Kraditor, Aileen S. *The Ideas of the Woman Suffrage Movement*. New York: Columbia University Press, 1965.

Langford, Gerald. *The Murder of Stanford White*. Indianapolis: Bobbs-Merrill Co., Inc., 1962.

Lankevich, George J., and Furer, Howard B. *A Brief History of New York*. New York: Associated Faculty Press, 1984.

Lawson, Anita. *Irwin S. Cobb*. Bowling Green, Ohio: Bowling Green State University Popular Press, 1984.

Marzolf, Marion. *Up from the Footnote: A History of Woman Journalists*. New York: Hastings House Publishers, 1977.

Marcuse, Maxwell. *This Was New York: A Nostalgic Picture of Gotham in the Gaslight Era*. New York: Columbia University Press, 1948.

May, Ernest R., and the Editors of Life. *The Progressive Era.* The Time-Life History of the United States, Vol. 9, 1901-1907. New York: Time, Inc., 1964.

Millard, Bailey, "What Life Means to Me," *Cosmopolitan Magazine* 41 (1906): 512-516.

Mooney, Michael MacDonald. *Evelyn Nesbit and Stanford White: Love and Death in the Gilded Age.* New York: William Morrow and Co., Inc., 1976.

Mott, Frank Luther. *American Journalism: A History of Newspapers in the United States Through 250 Years, 1690-1940.* New York: Macmillan, 1950.

Nesbit, Evelyn. *Prodigal Days.* New York: Julian Messner, Inc., 1934.

Nevins, Allan, and Krout, John A. *The Greater City: New York 1898-1948.* New York: Columbia University Press, 1948.

New York American. February 1–February 22, 1907.

New York Evening Journal. June 29, 1906–March 19, 1907, July 16, 1915, May 27, 1936, and January 17–19, 1967.

New York Evening World. June 26, 1906–October 31, 1919.

New York Journal and American. June 27, 1939.

New York Sun. February 24, 1907, and July 16, 1915.

New York Sunday Herald. April 5, 1902.

New York Telegraph. April 12, 1907.

New York Times. June 25, 1906, and June 5, 1902.

New York Tribune. November 2, 1902.

Patterson, Ada. *By the Stage Door.* New York: Grafton Press, 1902.

Pittsburgh Leader. April 10, 1907.

Riis, Jacob A. *How the Other Half Lives: Studies Among the Tenements of New York.* Cambridge, Mass.: Belknap Press, 1970.

Ross, Ishbel. *Ladies of the Press: The Story of Women in Journalism by an Insider.* New York: Harper and Brothers, 1936.

Ryan, Mary P. *Womanhood in America: From Colonial Times to the Present.* New York: F. Watts, 1983.

Sarasota Journal. June 27, 1939.

Schlipp, Madelon Golden, and Murphy, Sharon M. *Great Women of the Press.* Carbondale: Southern Illinois University Press, 1983.

Sinclair, Andrew. *The Better Half: The Emancipation of the American Woman.* New York: Harper and Row, 1965.

Smith, G. E. Kidder. *The Architecture of the United States.* New York: Anchor Books, 1981.

Sochen, June. *Herstory: A Woman's View of American History.* New York: Alfred Publishing Company, Inc., 1974.

Sochen, June. *Movers and Shakers: American Women Thinkers and Activists 1900-1970*. New York: Quadrangle/The New York Times Book Co., 1973.

Still, Bayrd. *Mirror of Gotham*. Westport, Conn.: Greenwood Press, 1980.

Tebbell, John. *The Compact History of the American Newspaper*. New York: Hawthorne Books, 1963.

Thaw, Evelyn. *The Story of My Life*. London: J. Long and Company, 1914.

Thaw, Harry K. *The Traitor. Philadelphia: Dorrance and Company, 1926.*

The Fabulous Century, by the Editors of Time-Life Books. Vols. 1-2. New York: Time-Life Books, 1969.

Toledo Blade. April 10, 1907.

Vanity Fair Magazine. New York: Vanity Fair Publishing Co., 1889-1913.

Wagenknecht, Edward. *American Profile: 1900-1909*. Amherst, Mass.: University of Massachusetts Press, 1982.

Wald, Lillian D. *The House on Henry Street*. New York: H. Holt and Co., 1915.

Who Was Who Among North American Authors. Detroit, Mich.: Gale Research Co., 1976.

Wilcox, Delos F. "The American Newspaper: A Study in Social Psychology," *Annals of the American Academy of Political and Social Science* 16 (July 1900): 56-92.

Yezierska, Anzia. *Bread Givers*. New York: Persea Books, 1975.

Yezierska, Anzia. *Hungry Hearts*. New York: Houghton-Mifflin Co., 1920.

Index

ABOUT THE AUTHOR

PHYLLIS LESLIE ABRAMSON, Ph.D., is President of the Abramson Group, Inc. in Atlanta, Georgia and is a professional speaker, lecturer, and consultant.